SCIENCE, CULTURE AND MAN

Science, Culture and Man

Impact of scientific progress on culture and human evolution

EDITED BY

Bepin Behari

Fellow of the Theosophical Society

FOREWORD BY

Hon'ble Justice B. P. Sinha

Chief Justice of India

MOTILAL BANARSIDASS

DELHI :: PATNA :: VARANASI

Bungalow Road, Jawaharnagar, Delhi-6.
Nepali Khapra, Varanasi U. P.
Bankipur, Patna (Bihar)

First Edition
1963

PRINTED IN INDIA BY SHANTILAL JAIN, SHRI JAINENDRA PRESS BUNGALOW ROAD, DELHI-6 AND PUBLISHED BY SUNDARLAL JAIN, MOTILAL BANARSIDASS, BUNGALOW ROAD, JAWAHARNAGAR, DELHI-6

DEDICATED

TO

THE LORD MAITREYA BODHISATTVA

I am glad to learn that you are issuing a collection of the addresses delivered at the Science Seminar last year which deals with the relationship between science and philosophy. Such a book will be very interesting and helpful. I am sorry I cannot send you a foreword for it, but you have my good wishes.

Jawaharlal Nehru

CONTENTS

PART III

FOREWORD

It is very gratifying that the Delhi Theosophical Federation is bringing out a series of talks given by eminent scholars and teachers on different aspects of human activity, with particular reference to the objective of the Theosophical Society to broaden human outlook and to bring home to humanity the ideal of universal brotherhood.

In India, ever since the dawn of history, we have not only been preaching but practising the high ideal of active toleration of all faiths and religious beliefs. We have also been aiming at the synthesis of spiritual values derived from thinkers of different schools of philosophy. It is, therefore, in the fitness of things that the late Dr. Rajendra Prasad, the first President of India for more than a decade, should have emphasized the concept of spiritual integration. It is also highly significant that the President of India, Dr. S. Radhakrishnan, a great philosopher and thinker that he is, should have laid special stress on the spriritual evolution of mankind from stage to stage, pointing out the ultimate consumation of that evolution into God-man. The Theosophists devoutly believe that we are all gods in the making. This volume contains other very thoughtful and thought-provoking talks which should be of considerable benefit to all those who are interested in the healthy growth of mankind as one Brotherhood. It is from that point of view that I welcome such a publication. May God grant it that this publication should serve the purpose it was intended to do !

Supreme Court of India, B. P. SINHA
New Delhi, the 1st September 1963 *Chief Justice of India*

PREFACE

These talks were delivered at the Science Seminar organized by the Maitreya Theosophical Centre, New Delhi; Dr. Rajendra Prasad and Dr. S. Radhakrishnan delivered their addresses on other occasions. These talks have been addressed mainly to theosophical audience. In modern age of great scientific stride but appalling moral and spiritual degeneration they may be of interest to general public as well.

These talks assume only preliminary knowledge of Theosophy. Ancient Wisdom diffused in almost all religious scriptures of the world is often concealed in myths and symbols. The Theosophical Society since it was founded in 1875 *in New York by Madame H. P. Blavatsky, Col. H. S. Olcott and others, has been trying to bring to light some of this hidden knowledge. But Divine Wisdom or Theosophy cannot be demarcated by any individual; this word has never at any time in the course of the history of the Society been officially defined. Each individual is expected to come to his own understanding of this Wisdom. Shri N. Sri Ram, the International President of the Theosophical Society, has however, suggested that "Theosophy may be regarded as the entirety of truth with regard to the whole process of the cosmos, comprehending every level of existence, and the significance of every phenomenon at each of these levels." On another occasion he said, "Theosopnhy is not so much a doctrine as a way of life, a way of thinking and feeling." Considered this way, Theosophy comprehends entire life, and no subject affecting any aspect of life is beyond the scope of its study. Both the scientists and the philosophers have vital role in discovering Theosophy which is "Wisdom undefined and unlimited".*

There are three Great Truths which are fundamental for understanding the nature of creation. These are : (1) God exists, and He is the great life giver who dwells within us and without us, is undying and eternally beneficient. He is not heard, nor touched, yet is perceived by the man who desires perception, (2) Man is immortal and his future is one whose glory and splendour have no limit, and (iii) a Divine Law of absolute justice rules the world so that each man is in truth his own judge, the dispenser of glory or gloom to himself, the decreer of his life, his reward, his punishment. Of the many corollaries that may be derived from these Great Truths, the laws of Karma and Reincarnation are very inspiring and consoling. They sustain the individual in days of his adversity; they provide him the bedrock for sane human relationship, and point out to him the way to right conduct.

These and many other teachings found in theosophical literature are believed in by a large number of members of the Theosophical Society. But this belief is not obligatory for membership of the Society. Its three declared objectives are (i) to form a nucleus of the Universal Brotherhood of Humanity, without distinction of race, creed, sex, caste and colour, (ii) to encourage the study of comparative Religion, Philosophy and Science and (iii) to investigate the unexplained laws of Nature and the powers latent in man. Those who are in sympathy with the first object of the Society may become its members.

The talks presented in this volume are divided

into three Sections. Part I *includes five talks devoted mainly to the problems of human relationship. It is through our relationship with others that we can be helpful and inspiring to them. On our attitude to life depends our relationship with others. Dr. Rajendra Prasad hoped that a synthesis between the material and the spiritual, between what we want and what we really need, between our physical and material requirements and our spiritual aspirations would enable India once again to give a kind of an object lesson to others. While indicating the need for establishing Universal Brotherhood, Dr. S. Radhakrishnan has emphasized that such Brotherhood cannot be established unless the very nature of man is transformed. Hon'ble Justice B. P. Sinha has indicated the goal of human evolution to be the salvation of mankind as a whole, to divinize man irrespective of his location, irrespective of his colour, irrespective of the belief that he holds. Prof. M. S. Thacker hopes that Science and Technology will usher in a beginning of an evolution of a close-knit federation of mankind the evolution of "One World". While dealing with the concept of the good life, Prof. K. G. Saiyidain has quoted the Holy Quran which says, "O God, give us the good things of this life and the good things of the life hereafter" implying thereby that there is no basic dualism between trying to live rich and full and complete life in the present and achieving good and virtuous life in future. The ideal of the Universal Brotherhood which is at the root of noble living, is very inspiring when the individual begins to live it; all other virtues follow this act of creative living; even culture and civilization will then flower in a natural way.*

Part II *considers the implications of the study of comparative Religion, Philosophy and Science. There are six talks included in this Section. No Study whether of Science or of Philosophy can really be useful unless it aids the individual and consequently his society in living a fuller life. For such a life, a radical revolution —mutation—in thought is necessary. Prof J. B. Rhine has amply demonstrated the need for a radical reorientation, consequent upon* psi *investigations, in our approach to the question of the nature of man. Prof T. R. Seshadri, F.R.S has sounded a positive note in suggesting close affinity between man's spiritual aspirations and his scientific discoveries. Indicating the relationship between Science, Philosophy and Religion, Prof. Seshadri has stated "Science deals with nature without and philosophy deals with nature within us, and religion deals with the manifestation of Divinity by controlling nature within and without." Prof. V. K R. V. Rao has affirmed the creative role of scientific investigations in preserving the essential Religion. He believes that "the march of science, so far as India is concerned, should not lead to the destruction of religion." Dr. S. Pradhan has shown that the ancient Indian religion and the modern scientific enquiries are mutually complementary. There is no basic difference between the two : in fact, "the word* Veda *and* Science *both have their roots in the terms meaning* Knowledge" *Acharya Shriman Narayan has argued that the religious approach to problems of the mundane world is neither contradictory to the scientific approach nor is it less effective as it is shown by the Gandhian approach to social problems. Shri T. V. R. Tatachari has pleaded for toleration for other man's faith and suspension of one's judgement in case one fails to understand the implications of some religious practices. A study of comparative Religion, Philosophy and Science suggests that there is no difference, fundamental or otherwise, between different ways of comprehending the laws of Nature and the immanence of One Universal Life. Such an understanding provides also the ethical basis of human conduct. It was Kabir who once stated that no one becomes a wise man merely by reading scriptures; wisdom is acquired by those who understand the real meaning of the simple word 'love'.*

Part III *of the book relates to the origin of life and the evolution of forms and consciousness. Although most of the theories discussed in this Section are common knowledge, yet these talks read together suggest inner depths in the pattern of evolution. There is a consciousness guiding the evolution of every atom of this universe. There is a pattern and rhythm in creation. There is an archetype to which every entity is progressing. From the subtlety of scientific investigations one is led to the understanding of the hidden side of things. The vast expanse of the cosmos transcends the limit of the physical sense-perception. Beyond the known, there is the limitless Unknown—though as real as the universe of the sense-perception. As one develops psychic powers and attains* siddhies, *veils after veils over one's consciousness are cast aside and the individual ultimately attains Perfection. There are many who believe in Perfected Humanity and the Adept Brotherhood. Shri J. P. Sanjana has discussed this problem very well in his talk* The Perfected Humanity. *Faith in the Perfected Humanity is difficult to inculcate, but once the significance of the Occult Hierarchy is rightly comprehended, our humanity will no longer remain "orphan". Those who are interested in this subject may pursue it on their own. Here we shall remain content merely by indicating that there is a vast literature on the subject for those who are genuinely interested. Rev. C.W. Leadbeater has written many useful books on the subject.*

We take this opportunity for thanking once again the speakers who participated in the Seminar, often at considerable inconvenience, and accorded permission for the publication of their talks. In response to our request, Prof. J. B. Rhine of the Duke University, North Carolina, U. S. A. sent us one of his very important papers on psi *investigations of which he is a pioneer. This paper was already published in the* Journal of Philosophy (*Dec.* 9, 1954), *but it very well demonstrates some of the theosophical teachings, so he readily agreed to its publication in the present volume. His Excellency Hon'ble Ellsworth Bunker, a former ambassador of the United States of America in India encouraged and helped us in many ways. Honble Justice B. P. Sinha, Chief Justice of India has always been ready to guide us in the theosophical and other philanthropic work. Shrimati Madhuri Behari has helped us in preparing the glossary and index. We acknowledge our gratitude to all these persons and to many others whose names have not been mentioned here but have been greatly helpful.*

The Maitreya Centre,
Delhi Theosophical Federation,
New Delhi, October 1, 1963.

BEPIN BEHARI

I

"Broaden instead of narrowing your sympathies; try to identify yourself with your fellows, rather than to contract your circle of affinity"

—The Master Koot Hoomi.

THE SPIRITUAL INTEGRATION

By

DR. RAJENDRA PRASAD
Late President of India

We have received our freedom now, but the problem of bringing about that kind of synthesis, which is required between the material and the spiritual, between what we want and what we really need, between our physical and material requirements and our spiritual aspirations, is still unsolved. It is this kind of synthesis, which we need and which movements like the theosophical movement alone can bring us. I, therefore, attach great importance especially in present conditions, when we see all around us the great strides which have been made by science in the material, technological and physical world. And when we see that although mankind has risen high in these respects, it has not been able to keep pace with the great attainments in matters spiritual and moral. And the result is a big chasm just in front of those who have marched so far and so fast. And that chasm is so big, so deep, that it can devour humanity unless mankind has the good sense, the wisdom and the foresight to see it and to jump it over. That can be done only by the realization of what we teach, what we preach. We need this kind of spritual realization to be able to see that after all what matters really is not what can be supplied from outside but what has to grow from within and thereby to fill the whole being of the individual. We want that synthesis, we want that knowledge and unless, as I have said, mankind rises to the times and sees the dangers ahead, mankind may be doomed. We are all thinking of wars and the terrible havoc and devastation which any new war will cause all the world over, and it will not only be a devastation but it may well be a total annihilation and with that prospect in view, we have to look for something which may turn us away from the direction in which we have been moving, into another more fruitful, more productive, more lasting, more helpful direction. And for that we need a spiritual background; for that we need an understanding which goes beyond material requirements and material comforts. And it is for this reason that people all the world over have been looking for something which will help them in this hour of great opportunities and of equally great, perhaps greater dangers. It is in that context that we have to approach all movements of the spiritual description, and as one interested generally in our welfare and in the welfare of mankind, I very often wonder, if India may not once again give a kind of an object lesson to others. In this country we have got all the faiths, we have got so many languages, and it is in this atmosphere of diversities which may appear to a superficial observer to be almost unconquerable, that we have to work for a synthesis and be it said that we have in the past succeeded in evolving that kind of synthesis. It may not have been a synthesis in the politicalsense or even in the material sense, but that we have been able to find the way of *Ahimsa* in the past, and it is only in that way that we can really make any progress at all. And if India has by adopting that course succeeded in winning freedom, it may as well place before the world, the same ideal for its acceptance, so that it may get freedom from all the risks, all the dangers, which are looming so large. In the present conditions we are not in a position to make that claim because we have not got the man of the hour at present. We have not got the courage to practise that in the way we would like it to be practised. We may lack even the wisdom to see far ahead but the background is there, the material is there, and may be that man may arise from amongst those who are engaged in these kinds of pursuits, who will be able to give the lead to his own country and through his own country to others also. It is in that hope that a man like me lives, and it is in that hope that I take every opportunity of going wherever I am wanted to go, so that I might perchance come across such a person, meet him face to face and draw inspiration from him.

TRANSFORM THE NATURE OF MAN

By

DR. S. RADHAKRISHNAN

President of India

We have been attempting to build universal brotherhood for a long time. Every great prophet has said that the world is one; it must be regarded as one family. But why is it that the League of Nations or the United Nations, these great organizations, which are intended to bring about a brotherhood, are not successful ? It is not possible for us to build universal brotherhood unless you transform the nature of man, unless you are able to depend not merely on external structures but on the inward soul, unless we are able to feel in the pulse of our being that we all belong to one human race; unless we are able to transcend our group loyalties and acknowledge the primacy of the human race.

That is one of the great ideals which we have had—to establish the universal brotherhood. And we rightly emphasize that such a brotherhood cannot be established unless it be on the plane of mind and spirit. We talk about comparative religion, but when we get behind any religion we discover that self-knowledge is the root of that religion. Get behind the doctrines, the rites, the ceremonies and all those other things which divide man from man; try to get to the bedrock of what we mean by religion. It is a deepening of your own awareness. It is self-knowledge. And it makes out that you cannot build a world of human brotherhood unless each individual becomes a transformer contributing to the raising of this great structure.

The laws of nature point out to you that there is something deeper than the world of space and time in which you live. If you open your eyes, you will discover that this progressive unfolding of the universe from matter to life, from life to animal mind, from animal mind to human intelligence, from human intelligence to God-man, to the spiritual soul, there has been a law governing this whole universe working in this devout consummation, namely turning over this earth into a true Kingdom of God, into a Brahma Loka, whatever you may call it.

That is the real purpose of human existence. If you do not acknowledge this spiritual dimension to your being, it will not be possible for you to work for this great principle. Whether it is the establishment of brotherhood, or study of comparative religion or the investigation of the laws of nature, you are putting them as three different objectives. They all come to the same thing that man is not merely a citizen of this world but he belongs to another world. His citizenship surely is rooted in heaven above. He has his roots in Heaven, his feet on earth. Unless we are able to recognize that spiritual character of our existence our life is mutilated; it is unfulfilled. For a truly human being one must recognize that besides his mental, physical, vital and intellectual nature, there is a spark of spirit in him which has to be fanned into a flame.

Our people therefore—all people—look upon religion as a changeover; changeover from the world of nature and necessity to the world of spirit and freedom; the displacement of *Avidya* by *Vidya*, the displacement of ignorance. When the Jains tell us 'Understand the nature of your ownself'; when the Buddha tells us 'Know what is not-self, everything which you cling to does not belong to what may be regarded as a true self'; when the Jews proclaim 'The spirit of man is the candle of Lord'; when the Christian affirms 'The kingdom of God is within you'; it is there when you penetrate behind your physical, mental, intellectual layer you will discover there the truth, the spark or the spirit. To recognize it, to stimulate it, to strengthen it, to let it permeate your whole being and make yourself a transformed creature—that is the purpose of human existence. All the different objectives ultimately come to this: Man requires to be changed, changed from his original nature to the nature of enlightenment —that is the purpose of religion.

Now, this is a time when we are not able to sit still; we are rushing from one thing to another. We listen to the radio, we go to the cinemas, read the newspapers, but we never have the patience to sit down, to sit still and reflect for ourselves. The greatest fruits of this world are the capacity to sit still, to meditate, to reflect, to read.

In this poisoned tree of *Samsara* there are two fruits which are nectar-like in their quality.

The tasting of the essence of great literature and communion with great souls, *Sallabha*, communion with great men, communion with great classics, these are the two inestimable fruits which this imperfect world of *samsara* offers us. By means of these two things, it will be possible for us to raise our own nature, to change ourselves. There is only one which is permanent in this world. That is the fulfilment of man's inner nature, through struggle, pain, toil and efforts. These are the things which discipline a man's mind, heart and soul and make him a changed being.

CULTURE AND BROTHERHOOD

By

HON'BLE JUSTICE B. P. SINHA

Chief Justice, Supreme Court of India, New Delhi.

In spite of what any particular scripture might say about the origin and genesis of the world, we know that life had been in existence for many millions of years. Of what we have now, we take many things for granted, but in ultimate analysis, we find that many things were discovered at great expense, not only of human efforts but of human life. The basic discovery of fire, the person whoever he might have been, was a greater discoverer than, I suppose, the discoverer these days of the atom bombs. We take fire for granted, but imagine the state of affairs when mankind did not know fire. Imagine the state of affairs when mankind did not know the art of agriculture. So the person, who made the invention of agritculture for the first time made a great contribution towards the human evolution, towards a great progress. We know that so long as agriculture was not invented mankind was fighting with the wild animals, fighting for his existence and striving simply to live. It is only agriculture which gave mankind the leisure to think of finer and better side of life.

The history of mankind, apart from the rise and fall of nations and kingdoms, has been the history of the expansion of human ideas with a view to conquering natural forces and harnessing those forces for the service of mankind. That in short, is the history of human efforts towards greater and better culture. So, I would define culture in the sense of the expanding ideas of mankind towards a fuller life in all its aspects, namely the aspects of fine arts, music, painting and other allied arts like architecture. All these have developed during so many, not only centuries but milleniums. Everyone, who claims the credit and we do not know who they were, of having invented each one of these items which collectively taken together make our culture possible, deserves to be remembered, though we very seldom think of them, taking as we do all these things taken for granted.

There is a dictum that 'There is no religion higher than Truth', and the efforts of mankind all round the path of history had been to discover that truth. The discovery of truth had led to the discovery of those hidden forces in nature, which lead us to the discovery of higher and higher truth. Therefore, the very complex development of society that we see now in our midst, the foundation of all these complexities was laid many many centuries ago and if those unknown heroes had not laid the foundation, then we would not have found our culture now.

It has rightly been said that the history of mankind is the history of expanded relationships between individuals and different units of mankind. If we think of mankind when they were living by themselves in jungles many many milleniums ago, after that they passed on to tribes, from tribes to families and from families to household economy and then to the village economy, through all these developments we find that they have reached the stage of nationalism, and from all these developments we have reached a stage where we are clamouring not only internationalism but universalism. All these are steps, the theosophists think, to the right direction. We are evolving to higher and higher life, and we are harnessing science and technology to that end.

The history of each branch of knowledge or science can be written in volumes. The person who invented the digits came from India. They say that it was India, the Hindasār, as the Arabians called it, where the higher mathematics began. Of course, later generations of mathematicians improved upon it. Recently, some scholars have revealed the wonders of the Vedic mathematics. I have heard an Indian scholar, a Swamiji claiming that there were 16 *sutras* in the Athrava Veda contained in an appendix which were aphorisms in a few words which the English translators could not understand because these did not yield any meaning simply by their word-meaning. But the Swami claimed that after years of researches these *sutras* have yielded keys to all higher mathematics. I am just referring to that to show that it has taken a great deal of efforts of mankind to search for and discover the latent truths, which were not open to us in the beginning but it now has laid them bare for us to study them. Therefore, we have to thank all those generations of scientists who have made possible for us to live a comfortable life that we are finding ourselves able to live. If you just think of mankind as they were, say, about eight thousand years ago, you will find that they must have had a much narrower outlook on life than we have today. The succeeding generations of man had an expanding outlook on life and to the extent they had been expanding their outlook on life, they have been going up and up in the scale of culture.

If you study each one of these several branches of knowledge and science, you will find not only that they are very much interrelated, but that all of them have been invented with certain ends in view, as the necessity is the mother of inventions. As occasions arose, mankind also rose equal to that occasion and made discoveries. Many discoveries were made during wars, and that illustrates that there is no unmixed good or evil. Even wars have led to many useful discoveries, and we have after these wars the benefits of these discoveries.

Technology has, of course, during the last hundred years made tremendous progress but as I said before, the foundation of these changes was laid by scientists who had come thousands of years earlier. Culture, as I understand, means therefore, the accumulated knowledge of mankind thoughout the ages and the expanding outlook of mankind with reference to each one of these forces of knowledge which have yielded results in science, arts and in technique, which all collectively have yielded what we call culture. True culture is that culture which will lead mankind into one organization. Therefore, we find that the great poet Robindranath Tagore who sang in the beginning of the twentieth century sang of the whole mankind as one unit; he sang so when most of the so called advanced countries of Europe were fighting for nationalism; at that time each country was against the other. The great poet said that when you talk of nationalism you are really creating a rift among the different sections of mankind whereas you must think of the whole mankind. It is only by going beyond these national barriers that we can make any real progress.

Culture, therefore, in my view means that men should look to the entire mankind as one unit. The effort made by any individual is an effort made in the interest of the whole mankind, each one is making individual contribution to the collective whole, which we characterise by the name of culture. From that standpoint, I think, we can claim a larger share towards the evolution and towards the consumation of the ideal for which we all are working—towards the ideal of the salvation of mankind as a whole irrespective of his location, irrespective of his colour, irrespective of the beliefs that he holds; because after all, true culture does not recognize such an artificial division. Culture in a word, overrides castes, and in my humble opinion, we are all working towards that noble end. Let us end this with our praying to God that He may give us, all mankind, the widsom to work in right direction and to think for the salvation of mankind.

TECHNOLOGICAL PROGRESS AND CULTURE

By

PROFESSOR M. S. THACKER

Member, Planning Commission

(Former Director General, Council of Scientific & Industrial Research, Government of India, New Delhi)

Many of you may be aware of what has come to be called the Vienna Declaration of September 19, 1958, in which seventy leading scientists from twenty countries have expressed their hopes and fears regarding recent developments in technology and their impact on civilization and culture. These intellectuals called upon the scientists and technologists of the world to pool their capacities for the constructive use of science to better serve the common interests of mankind.

This is a significant statement. It has highlighted the power that technology has come to possess on the affairs of mankind. Not that this recognition is new—for technology has always exercised this influence—but recent developments have given it an importance, —may be out of fear, may be out of hope—which has forced itself on the people all over the world.

What is this technology ? And how does it affect society and culture ? Viewing from a broad perspective, culture may be taken as the resultant of inherited ideas, habits and values, of arts, crafts and material prosperity. Man continuously alters his surroundings in order 'to live' and creates, inevitably a secondary environment. If man had depended only on his anatomical equipment, he would have perished long ago out of hunger and exposure. He equips himself with gadgets which enable him to act effectively and to protect himself against the dangers to which he is exposed. This creative activity, this creation of 'artefacts', has been going on all the time, and even in the most primitive stages, man had to equip himself for his defence, food, movements, and so on. These were inherited by succeeding generations and improved upon and added to. This material outfit of man—his dwellings, his implements and weapons, and so on, constitute the tangible aspects of his culture. And all these were created to serve a purpose from selected available materials according to certain techniques. They could not have been devised on the basis of mystic and non-empirical conceptions. Knowledge was necessary for their production and use; and such knowledge should have been based on careful observations of materials constituting his environment, on reasoning, and generalisations; and these are the essential facets of scientific inquiry. This knowledge which forms the basis of material culture is a complement to the whole body of intellectual discipline consisting of moral, spiritual and economic values, of social organization and language. Anthroplogists recognize artefacts and customs as the two fundamental aspects of culture. As Malinowski puts it :

"Culture is essentially an instrumental reality which has come into existence to satisfy the needs of man in a manner for surpassing any direct adaptations to the environment; man has his wants as an implement-making and implement-using creature, as a communicating and discoursing member of a group as the guardian of a traditional continuity, as a family unit within a co-operative body of men, as one who is haunted by the past or in love with it, as one whom the events to come fill with hopes and anxieties, and finally as one to whom the division of labour and the provisions for the future have given leisure and opportunities to enjoy colour, form and music".

Having said that techniques and science have always contributed to the culture of man, it is easy to appreicate that their effectiveness has been a measure of various cultural levels in the progress of mankind. I am not suggesting that primitive man had recognized the importance of techniques and science or their inter-relationship. All that I wish to emphasize is that what we now recognize and designate as technology and science have been put to use by man from the earliest times and that they have influenced his activities, social organization and culture through the ages.

This statement needs elaboration. Early techniques were developed solely by trial-and-error processes. Advances were slow and were made by those who had little or no education as we today understand it. Nevertheless, contrary to the common belief, many notable steps in technical progress had been taken long before the Industrial Revolution. From a technological point of view, all human history hinges upon two revolutions, the neolithic passage from hunting to agriculture and the modern passage from agriculture to industry. The first was the longest, from the time of man's advent on this planet up to about seven thousand years ago. According to several scholars, about one-third of the techniques that are now in use belong to this period. A great deal was learned about the elements with which man came into contact—animals and plants required for food and the material objects in the surroundings. The techniques of hunting, trapping and taming of animals; dressing of hides and skins; working in stones, wood and bone; cooking; drawing and painting—all these were learned by the hard way. The gradual development of society and language also belongs to that period, and all these constituted the essential preparations for the great revolution in human society ushered in by agriculture.

It has been rightly said that civilization—by which is meant, to use Will Durant's words : a vague complex of order and provision, manners and morals, culture and comfort—started with agriculture. Perhaps, it started somewhere in Southern Turkistan and spread eastwards to China, southwards to India, and westwards to Elam, Sumeria and Egypt. By about 4,000 B.C. the River Valley Civilizations were flourishing in quite a few regions. The importance of the agricultural civilization to us, in the context of the present discussion, lies in its making possible, for the first time, the development of the social institutions of villages and towns, and of trade. The technique of spinning and weaving, and of pottery and use of metals, are associated with it. Communities settled in villages and engaged in tilling and other agricultural operations produced surpluses which could be bartered for tools and implements, and articles of luxury, produced by craftsmen settled in towns. Transport to distant places became necessary and accounts had to be maintained. Measures and numbers had to be improvised and standardized, and records had to be maintained. Long before the rise of the classical Greek civilization houses of stone, wood and brick; wheeled vehicles and sailing craft; and even simple machines, like the inclined plane, the pulley and the lathe, had been developed. This is not all. The rise of towns had another consequence; there arose a class of people—the priestly class—with their essential requirements provided for and with enough leisure and curiosity to indulge in intellectual persuits. Several useful developments in astronomy, arithmetic, algebra and medicine can be traced to the preclassical period. But it is worthy of note that the intellectual class got divorced from the craftsmen who were left to produce the essential needs of society unaided. Science and technology pursued their independent courses and while the latter was geared closely to the material needs of the people, the priestly class assumed to itself a position of knowledge and authority and its views and formulations were imbibed into social fabric and transformed with additions and modifications to be further elaborated by subsequent generations.

It would take us too long to wade through tangled history and present a continuing study of the impact of technology on cultural developments. It should be emphasized, however, that the contacts between science and technology were few and tenuous, even after the Renaissance. The craftsmen were essentially utilitarians and they devised and developed methods and techniques based on materials available to them and thereby significantly contributed to the improvement and expansion of material culture.

The progress of science during this long period up to the Renaissance and the Industrial Revolution in Europe which followed it, was by no means even; nor was it confined to any particular region. The decline of pastoral civilization in the eastern River Valleys of Asia was followed by the spectacular rise of Hellenistic science which flourished for about a thousand years and then withered. The knowledge developed by the Greeks migrated to the East which reinforced by contributions from Arab countries, India and China, re-entered Europe and prepared the ground for the great Renaissance. It may be noted, however, that despite all its intellectual brilliance and dazzle, the science of the Classical period, did not make any substantial contribution to the practical and material realities of life. The Greek scholars disdained practical applications. But the prestige which went with Greek science had a dynamism which was responsible for its spreading far and wide, from the Atlantic to the Hindukush, and it influenced the ideas and thoughts of peoples over vast areas. Throughout the so-called Middle Ages, civilizations were flourishing in Asia, and contacts among them, particularyly through trade, increased progressively. Manufacturing techniques improved, especially in weaving, pottery and metal work. Many inventions in mechanics and navigation were made and introduced into Europe before the Italian Renaissance.

The broad base on which historical events are founded, should not be lost sight of. Regional designations of such events are likely to convey the false impression that such developments are confined to any one people or within strict chronological limits. History does not divide itself neatly into a series of ages that one finds described in textbooks. Every development has taken place as a result of preparatory endeavours that are going on continuously, and the peoples inhabiting various regions have contributed to it. When we speak of the Italian Renaissance or the subsequent Industrial Revolution in Britain, we mean a transition from the Middle Ages to the Modern Age which manifested first in certain regions and later spread into other countries which were prepared for it. The Renaissance which ushered expansive and progressive forces, implied a new conception of the material world. The revival of learning, the application of printing for the diffusion of knowledge, and the geographical discoveries opened out new possibilities for the people, who had found strength in their own abilities after shaking off the crippling shackles of ecclesiastical and feudal despotism. The mental barriers of medieval orthodoxy were broken and the best minds in Europe were prepared for speculative adventures. Invention, as it were, was on a spree. The balance of technological superiority had swung gradually from the East to the West. European commercial intrusion into the East and its supremacy in military matter then—made possible by the seamen's compass and the gun powder, both of which were taken from outside—gave Europe advantages which were fully utilized. The crafts of Asian civilization, which combined artistic excellence and refinement, were absorbed; and ideas from whichever source they were to be had, were utilized. Expanding markets stimulated technical improvements aimed at improving the output; large production inspired search for new markets. With rising opulence, money was readily available for experiment and investment in manufacturing enterprises. Factories using machinery and power were started and the age of artisans and craftsmen was coming to a close.

The impact of these developments on traditional concepts of creation and evolution was even more revolutionary than that on economic productivity, as they concern the very foundations of beliefs held by mankind. The dislodgement of the earth from the centre of the universe to a planetary position of one of the suns, the celestial mechanics of Newton, the origin of species and organic evolution through natural selection, and the overthrow of the principle of spontaneous, generation may be mentioned as instances.

This narration is rather over simplified account of the procession of events which led to the Industrial Revolution, that is, to the emergence of a social order in which machinery and power, international trade and commerce suppplanted an order characterised by pastoral occupations and local markets. The causes which led to the Industrial Revolution have been discussed by scholars and abundant literature exists on this subject. It took place first in England in the eighteenth century and later, spread to other countries; industrial revolution is still taking place in some others. Wherever it has taken place the course of change has been roughly similar; textile production was usually the first to be affected, then the making of metal articles and foodstuffs; the large-scale production of iron and steel was a distinct step; and the manufacture of machines and producers' goods came last. The transformation to industrial societies from peasant societies was not brought about without strife and discontent, and the remedies applied to mitigate them are more or less the same all over, and this has tended to standardize occupations, working hours and even the amusements of man in industrial societies.

The Industrial Revolution was primarily a result of the upsurge in technological inventions. But the factor which invested technology with dynamism, particularly as the change gaind momentum, was science. I have stated before that the progress of science followed, from the beginning of the pastoral civilization, a path distinct from that of techniques. Practical experience of craftsmen had been accumulating for centuries, and ingenuity provided the motive force for the development of such processes as the dyeing of cloth, preparation of soap, glass and gun-powder, tanning of leather and extraction of metals from ores. Even the invention of the textile mill and the steam engine is the result of empirical trial-and-error processes and such activities benefited vastly by the spirit of experiment which was characteristic of the time. Technique had much more to give to science than they could learn from it. This was well recognized by the scientists themselves. The founders of the Royal Society of London, for instance, pleaded for the close association of science and technology and emphasized that both stood to benefit by such association.

The nineteenth century saw a phenomenal expansion in the content and scope of science, and industrial development was beginning to be materially influenced by science. From its passive role of 'investigating nature', science entered the phase of 'effecting all things possible'. The integration of science into production mechanism was itself an effect of the industrial Revolution. Science proliferated into separate sub-sciences and began to probe deeply into various fields and produced results which were seized upon and utilized for productive enterprises. The science of electricity played a vital part in the revolution of communications. The internal combustion engine had a similar effect on transport. The chemical industry had permeated agriculture and medicine. The initiative for invention gradually passed from the ingenious inventor to the scientist and development of engineer. Deliberate and systematic invention came into the picture and isolated inspiration and empirical fumbling began to count less and less. By joining technology, science raised the ceiling of technical achievement and widened the field for industrial enterprise. As pointed out by the great philosopher A. N. Whitehead, the greatest invention of the nineteenth century was that of the "power to invent".

Technological changes have a global import and may be regarded as a progressive fulfilment of the changes initiated by the Industrial Revolution; with gathering momentum, the speed of change and the geographical spread have increased. Towards the close of the last century, technology had already profoundly influenced economic and social life in Europe and America; Asia and Africa were comparatively unaffected. Towards the close of the first World War, Japan had emerged as an industrial power. Today, America and USSR hold dominant positions, China and India are getting into the stride of industrialization. Quite a number of countries which are now considered 'undeveloped' or 'underdeveloped' are considering plans of development. All countries, in one way or another, get involved in the spread of industrialization; even the response to demands for raw materials from industrial countries created changes in the patterns of life. The sinking of oil wells in the deserts of Middle East—and they have already sunk in Sahara—and the construction and maintenance of pipelines, for instance, have worked remarkable changes to the people in the concerned regions, as pointed out in a recent issue of *Impact*. "The labour required can only be recruited from nomadic herdsmen. They forsake their tents, live in houses and villages, become familiar with the amenities and frustrations of urban life and learn technical processes. Beliefs and customs accepted for centuries may be abandoned in the process, tribal systems destroyed and authority undermined to give place to a somewhat colourless existence without faith or objective beyond economic gain." Anyone who has seen the transformations in the large areas in India surrounding the mighty steel projects and colossal multi-purpsose river dams, will have an idea of the impact of technology on the social, cultural and educational life of the people.

Thus when we come to the present century, we find technology in an invigorated and expansive state, permeating every phase of human activity. In the past techniques were evolved by trial-and-error processes to meet certain requirements demanded by society. In the present phase technology anticipates problems, finds solutions for them, and creates demands for new products and materials. By overt involvement in the two world wars, it has demonstrated its powers for destruction in a manner which has staggered public imagination. The first war centred round the chemical industry. In the second, the dominant technology was based on physics and new weapons were designed and developed, and among them the atom bomb. Modern aircraft, radar, electronic instrumentation, and the generation of nuclear power, these and many others owe their elaboration to the impact of war. On the chemical side, the development of antibiotics and pesticides, which have had so much influence on public health and agriculture, also emerged from the war crucible. The war gave impetus to the new technique of operational research which has applications to the analysis and understanding of complex situations involving large numbers of variables.

These and other developments have demonstrated the universal possibility of applying science and technology for the formulation and solution of industrial, agricultural and health problems; they have also shown that they can be applied for military adventures—hydrogen bombs, radioactive and bacteriological poisons, and so on, catering to the pugnacity of man. Today, industries and governments are increasingly dependent on technology, and the people everywhere are becoming conscious of its power as an agent of political and social transformation. This is a development of the same order of crucial significance as the emergence of civilization itself. There is one difference; the pace of this change is rapid, and while in the past, the process was slow and was spread over several generations, the present change is much more rapid in relation to the life-span of man. The transformation of industry through science and technology may be said to have had a real start only in the early years of the present century; already the evolution of production methods have reached a stage when automation, in which complex operations in their entirety are performed without human control, is being seriously considered. Nuclear fission was thought of only a couple of decades ago; now electric power is being generated on a commercial scale in some countries and more recent developments indicate that the fear of power shortage is likely to be annulled for ever. New consumer goods created by technology are becoming ubiquitous. They have entered the every day life of the citizen—in the routine of cooking and washing, music, art, hobbies and entertainment, care of children, transport and communication, preservation of health and physical fitness, and so on.

It is not merely the pace, but also the magnitude of change that characterize the twentieth century technology, which has verily become an industry of invention. Every increase in its output tends to activate known results and brings out new applications, that is, the impact of a new invention is not just cumulative, but catalytic. It creates new industries and new demands for industrial products. The president of a leading chemical corporation in U.S.A. estimates that half the working force in that country is engaged in producing and selling goods unknown fifty years ago; he further estimates that half the working force will be similarly concerned with products as yet unkown.

It will be clear from what I have said, that technology, by its own achievements has moved into a controlling position in the social sphere. So massive and so penetrating are these achievements, that fear has been expressed in some quarters that technological knowledge and experience in handling nature's material and force have arrived too soon—much in advance of the capacities of cultural, economic, and political institutions to absorb them. The question is asked whether men and communities can adapt themselves to the new situation in which drastic changes in environments are created by technology. Many thinkers aver that the material power of man has outrun his moral stature and that the civilization which he himself created over ages stands in peril.

There is no gainsaying that such doubts and fears have been occasioned by the destructive potentialities of nuclear weapons. It is possible to get things out of focus if we think of technology in terms only of the atom bomb. True, the revelations of Hiroshima and Nagasaki have given ample cause for horror, but the very appreciation of the holocaust has induced much rethinking on the possibilities of deterring the misuse of knowledge which technology has placed at man's disposal.

Technology is primarily concerned with human betterment. It points the way to do things better—a revolt against static order. "Knowledge is power" is an old adage, and among the powers that knowledge confers is also the power to do ill. In modern technology, there is much of such knowledge; there is much more that can be employed for the good, and its use only for the good is ensured by the exercise of collective social wisdom. The history of technology shows that the interaction between technology and society has been intimate and reciprocal, and that social forces have determined that course of technological advance. Technology has become a part of the production forces of society, and there is no question of condemning or rejecting it. The culture of every age is dominated by certain overtones; and today, the dominant overtone is technology.

I have referred to in this talk impact of technology on society. If I may define culure rather crudely—it is an amalgam of inherited customs, manners, habits, attitudes towards life, beliefs and philosophies; it includes the prevalent traditions and the arts and crafts which flourish in particular societies. It is the concomitant result built up by the tendencies and efforts of generations of groups of people. I would like to lay stress on two particular features of culture; one is that it is shared by a whole community of people and that it is not the peculiar monopoly of individuals. Tendencies and influences, which are acceptable to the collective wisdom of the people are allowed to mould and shape the culture of the society.

The other feature of culture to which I may refer to is that it is never static; it is a growing organism, changing sometimes for the better, sometimes for the worse, but ever changing. Each generation inheriting a certain culture, contributes in its own way to it.

There are several types of culture one hears of. Various groups of societies of people have been flourishing in different parts of the world, and each society has been following a well-knit pattern of its own. History records the mutual influence of different cultures whenever they came into contact with each other. Sometimes there have been serious cultural conflicts.

Today, it is no longer possible for any one society to live in complete isolation from the rest of the world. Rapid means of communication have annihilated distance and the world has visibly shrunk. I hope, a common culture of man will emerge as a result of close contacts between various societies of the world. And I also hope that Science and Technology will usher in a beginning of an evolution of a close-knite federation of mankind, the evolution of "One World".

THE CONCEPT OF THE GOOD LIFE

By

PROF. K. G. SAIYIDAIN

Former Education Secretary,
Government of India, New Delhi.

When we speak of the good life, we are really defining a certain comparative stituation of adjustment. We live in an environment which is always changing, but there are certain values which do not change, certain ideas which do not alter. It has been our endeavour throughout that the individuals adjust and adapt themselves in such a way that a balance is maintained between that which changes and that which is permanent. But the rate of change during the last two hundred years or so had been so rapid that, even to maintain one's position, as some one remarked in *Alice in the Wonderland*, one has to keep on running. This question becomes important because all the projects and schemes of national development that we adopt must be envisaged as for a better and fuller life. It is men who are not means but ends in themselves. So, in discussing this theme, we are at the crux of the human problem and what our Prime Mnister once called "investment in man".

There have been many forces in the last couple of hundred years which, broadly speaking, are not favourable for the growth of the good life of our hopes. But even these forces could be used for man's advancement and growth; it depends upon our human understanding and our compassion and sympathies with our fellow-beings.

During the last so many years, specially since the beginning of the present century, there have been the two global wars and in between them and even after the second world war there has been the period of troubled and uneasy peace—a kind of mental and emotional distrubance which is very harmful and detrimental for the human development. During this period there also developed many aggressive nationalistic and racial trends which gave a set-back to human progress. I am thinking at the moment, specially of movements like Nazism and Fascism, and racial fanaticism as it is practised in the South Africa. The facile optimism of H.G. Wells predicting a kind of continuous, unbroken peaceful progress depending on science and general enlightenment has been to a considerable extent, denied by the changes that took place in the second decade of the present century.

There has been another strong force working against the good life and human progress. This is the tremendous and glaring economic inequalities which have existed not only among different countries but among the different communities of the same country. This is very unhealthy because it tends to cut the individual off from the creative stream of life. The spirit of humanity cannot thrive either in excessive riches or in glaring poverty. Under those circumstances the individuals and groups are not only faced with so many wasteful conflicts, but man is unable to develop proper cultural values. On account of inner and outer tensions it becomes difficult, if not impossible, for a normal person to develop humane values or proper cultural and moral attachments. Moreover, the concentration of power in a few hands leads to cruel exploitation, both political in the sense of colonialism and economic in the sense of the exploitation of material resources for the benefit of a few. You will find that, as a result of scientific developments and discoveries, there has been a large-scale exploitation of the means of production. Its results, however have not been used for the good of the people but for the advantage of a small section of the people or for the personal gain of those who have power to control and exploit, though in this century the area of this group has expanded under various pressures. Such exploitive activities can never be useful for the good life.

In more recent years, as a result of the great explosion of knowledge, specially as a result of the nuclear fission, man has got an insight into the mysteries of nature; even the unseen and unsuspected energy of atoms and protons has been brought under human knowledge and control. Science, which is a great achievement of man, has given him so much knowledge and power that it has become possible for him for the first time either to enrich man's life beyond imagination or to wipe out the whole of mankind. So, today, we have tremendous power in the hands largely of those who do not know how to use it and, therefore, the destructive aspect of the science has come to the forefront.

Then, there have been various illiberal movements which deny the value of democracy. There are those who consider the State as more important than the individual, and the collective good is taken to be of such colossal importance that in its pursuit they will readily sacrifice the individual who is the spring of all cultural values. These persons obviously work against the very bases of the human progress. Such movements which deny the value of democracy can be converted among forces which stand against the progress of mankind.

Finally, on account of the tremendous technological development and new ranges of speed and movement as well as a general increase in the tempo of life, tension for the individual is also increasing and everyday life has become much more complex. When we compare the life in bigger cities with that in smaller towns and villages, between countries like the United States and India, we find that one of the consequences of the new technological development has been an absence of harmonious development of the individual and his satisfactory adaptation to his environment. Today, the centre of man's life is tending more and more *outside* him. What the sages and *rishies* of the past thought should be inwards is tending to turn more and more outward and, therefore we depend for our happiness more and more on "prefabricated amusements". Thus, the centre of our spiritual life is not so much inward as outward. As a result of this we go to cinemas, bull-fights, or take to drinks and other similar amusements so that these different forms of diversions may cover up the impoverishments of our inner spiritual life. This is how we seek to divert our minds from our really impoverished existence.

These are some of the forces operating against the growth and development of mankind in the present age, but they can be transformed into beneficial forces if they are rightly used. They could enable us to have all our basic necessities easily satisfied. Now, distance and time have been controlled and conquered to a very great extent. It is possible even for ideas to travel with the speed of thought. Science is also helping in evolving better methods of production. Mechanical means have been developed to such an extent that it is for the first time that the world is entering the realm of plenty, and, if this opportunity is rightly utilized, the leisure thus attained could be of infinite value to the mankind at large.

The question of democracy has acquired a new significance in recent years. In spite of all the atrocities of the nineteenth century there has developed a greater concern for the common man, which has been increasingly emphasized both during the last and the present century. The importance and concern for social justice has also greatly increased. It is requried now, not for any particular group or class but, for society as a whole. The good life is now visualized in terms of the entire people. So, when we think of building up a new world, it is obvious that social organization should not be based on exploitation. Adquate provision of the basic needs of life must be made for every one—that is what social justice emphasizes. Many Prophets, religious leaders and social thinkers have been always saying that material riches should be secured for all, but it is only now that it has become *possible* to hope to provide them to *every* one to share the good things of life with all.

In the new type of the world that we are trying to build, there should be real freedom of expression which is very often denied. This means the very denial of what is the birth-right of every individual. When freedom of expression is denied, it means the very spirit of mankind is denied. In the new social order each individual must have the opportunity to express himself and to live a creative life without any undue restriction. We should use the power that is given by science creatively so that every individual can lead a happy and harmonious life.

What is the content of this good life and what are the essential conditions which must be fulfilled so that the good life is universal and not the monopoly of a few individuals or any select group !

There should be real and constructive peace —peace for doing creative work in which men's latent creative capacities can find the fullest expression. So long as the fear of nuclear warfare hangs on mankind, it cannot apply its mind to creative work.

Secondly, democracy which has been established in many countries should be broadened so that it is not only political but also social and cultural democaracy. Such a state of affairs is necessary for the growth and development of the inner man—man who, as the famous philosopher Kant said, "is an end in oneself, not a means for something else". Thus democracy, based on social justice becomes our beacon light.

Lastly, there must be an equitable sharing of material and cultural goods. The concept of the good life should be so broad that it includes both the material and the spiritual aspects of life. It has oscillated during the past rather violently between materialism and asceticism. Often it has been held that the happiness of an individual or a nation is synonymous with the amount of the material goods they possess. This is one view point. On the other hand, there is a viewpoint which is said to have prevailed in the East—although I do not really subscribe to any sharp antithesis between the East and the West in this regard—that the good life is the life of asceticism, that the real meaning of life is to be found in the life of a recluse, the life of withdrawal. Sheikh Sadi in a poem aptly differentiated between the man of learning and the ascetic; between the scholar and the man of religion. He said that the man of learning is not primarily interested in saving himself, whereas the ascetic is interested in saving himself, his own soul. One tries "to salvage his own blanket", the other "to save the drowning man". If you withdraw from this material world, you withdraw yourself from the basic raw material of life. No man in this interdependent world can save his soul without working co-operatively. In fact, in order to have a full and rich life, one must live in this world with all its trials and difficulties. This attitude of material and spiritual synthesis was described very well by a Muslim philosopher by saying that you should develop mental and emotional 'detachment' which will give you such integrity and courage that when the world is conquered and is lying at your feet, you are not ensnared by it. Nor can the good life, however, be built on the basis of material deprivations. It would be unsuitable and unrealistic to think that an ordinary man can develop the good life or moral and spiritual values, unless proper material conditions are secured. In the Holy Quran there is a phrase which I would like to share with you because it gives a synthesis of the two values. It says, "O God, give us the good things of this life and the good things of the life hereafter", meaning thereby that there is no basic dualism between trying to live rich and full and complete life in the present and achieving the good and virtuous life for the hereafter. You must sow here what you are to reap hereafter. This idea has been repeated in almost all the important religions of the world like Hinduism, Buddhism, Sikhism and Christianity. It has been well-said in one of the scriptures that he who is blind in this world will also be blind in the next. Unless you have a good life here, you cannot have a good life there.

Developments of science and the means of transport have reduced the size of the world. It has become "One world" as Wendel Wilkie has called it; someone else called it 'The world is my village'. It is not possible now for any country to continue to live alone, in complete isolation from the rest of the world. A flood, an epidemic or any natural catastrophe becomes an international problem. Since the world has become "a neighbourhood", it is necessary to cultivate and exercise neighbourly feelings towards all. So we should develop an enormous sense of social responsibility.

The "good life" should be envisaged not for the individual himself or his nation but for the world as a whole.

One other important thing we should bear in mind. In the world of future where the good life prevails, man will not live by bread alone, but equally he will not live without a good measure of bread. It was Mahatma Gandhi who said that to the poor man even God comes in the form of bread. In fact, for the blossoming of the 'good life' in every heart, it is essential to blend properly the material and the spiritual cravings of man. In this context, I would like to share with you a quotation of great beauty entitled "Not by Bread Alone".

"Man does not live by bread alone, but by beauty and harmony, truth and goodness, work and recreation, affection and friendship, aspiration and worship.

"Not by bread alone, but by the splendour of the firmament at night, the glory of the heavens at dawn, the blending of colours at sunset, the loveliness of magnolia trees, the magnificence of mountains.

"Not by bread alone, but by the majesty of ocean breakers, the shimmer of moonlight on a calm lake, the flashing silver of a mountain torrent, the exquisite patterns of snow crystals, the creations of artists.

"Not by bread alone, but by the sweet song of a mocking-bird, the rustle of the wind in the trees, the magic of a violin, the sublimity of a softly lighted cathedral.

"Not by bread alone, but by the fragrance of

roses, the scent of orange blossoms, the smell of newmown hay, the clasp of a friend's hand, the tenderness of a mother's kiss.

"Not by bread alone, but by comradeship and high adventure, seeking and finding, serving and sharing, loving and being loved.

"Man does not live by bread alone, but by being faithful in prayer, responding to the guidance of the Holy Spirit, finding and doing the loving will of God now and eternally.

II

"Lead the life necessary for the acquisition of such knowledge and powers, and wisdom will come to you naturally."

—*H. P. Blavatsky*

THE SCIENTIFIC OUTLOOK

By

PROF. S. PRADHAN, D. SC.

Indian Agricultural Research Institute, New Delhi.

One can speak on the scientific outlook of so many aspects of everyday life but in the present context it is most appropriate to throw some light on the scientific outlook of religion. I am a student of biology and having studied the physics and chemistry of life, I feel all the more convinced that there is no opposition between science and religion. Science is not opposed to philosophy either; there is a definite philosophy behind every branch of science and philosophy cannot endure long without scientific supports.

There has been a feeling that a scientist cannot be a religious person; a scientist is generally considered an atheist. This controversy between science and religion is, however, not of Indian origin. Wherever religion constitutes a set of fixed theories any expression of questioning attitude raises a lot of storm. This has been so specially with regard to the theory of evolution. When the scientist began propounding this theory, it was taken specially in the West as a challenge to the authority of the scriptures. So the scientists were considered irreligious. As far as India is concerned, this has not been her attitude. In this country there has been the tradition of constant enquiry into Truth; repeated discussions on scriptures have given rise to different schools of thought which have made this country profound in religious and spiritual matters.

Obviously, science is not religion, but fundamentally there is no difference between these two approaches to the fact of life. This is the theme I am trying to present. Let us take up the various aspects wherein science and religion appear to differ from each other, and let us examine whether there is any real difference between the two.

It is often said that religion consists of beliefs and faiths whereas science is concerned with facts and observations. Liberty to question the authority is said to be the special privilege which only scientists enjoy. It is not a fact. The Indian religious tradition is full of examples of religious conferences and discussions wherein the learned *pundits* of various schools assembled to discuss together and to arrive at the right understanding of Truth. This was the practice among the Hindus and this was common among the Buddhists too. These conventions were held not for mutual appreciation but they were organized to discuss at times fiercely, to question frankly and to arrive authoritatively at definite interpretations and right understanding of the fundamental tenets of religion. There is no point in citing examples of such religious seminars between scholars when we find in the Bhagavad Gita that Arjun put so many rather discomforting questions to the Lord Himself. This Gita is considered as one of the most revered scriptures of India and yet it is not very much different from any learned discussion among the scientists.

It should be appreciated that one has to act on some belief or faith even in science at every stage. When you switch on the light your action is based on the belief in the work of Faraday and those who followed up his scientific investigations; you do not experiment every time. In the same way there is some element of belief in all the conclusions of science once they are arrived at by authorities in whom people have developed faith. You believe them; you do not repeat their experiments again and again. Similarly when the theologists arrived at certain conclusions they put them in scriptures and these conclusions are documented as religious tenets. These conclusions are valid as those of scientists. So in science and in religion both there is respect for reason as well as there is scope and necessity for belief. Occasionally young students of science are asked to take for granted, for the time being, certain intricate scientific principles which they are not equipped to understand at the moment. Thus in science also as in religion there is sometimes the necessity to keep one's questioning attitude in abeyance till one is ready to understand the question and the answer.

It has been pointed out by some people that the scientists' approach to the quest for Truth is through experiments whereas the philosopher approaches his problem through contemplation. This again is a merely superficial difference. In religion too, one observes, notes, collects data, which of course may be through one's eyes, ears or through other sense-organs, but nonetheless, one observes and having made these observations one begins to think. Observation and contemplation go together in science as well as in religion; one without the other is ineffective. The scientist Sir James Jeans has emphasized the relationship between collection of data and contemplation over them so much that according to him a large collection of data without contemplation is like a large heap of bricks for the man who wants to build the house. Just as physical organization of bricks makes the house, the mental arrangement of the data is necessary for arriving at any conclusion. Sir Jagdish Chandra Bose, the eminent Indian scientist, gave the first place to meditation and the next to experimentation which in fact is the Eastern way. The Western way generelly prefers meditation to follow experimentation. Whether we approach the problem from the Eastern or the Western way, the experiments or the observations of data and meditation both are absolutely necessary for the search after Truth.

It is very often said that there is use of intelligence in science and use of intuition in religion. This also is not quite correct. In fact we do not know enough either about intuition of about intelligence. It is said that the lower animals work on instinct, scientists with intelligence, and philosophers and religious seers on intuition. What is the difference between instinct, intelligence and intuition ? We do not perceive the actual processes through which instinct works, and so is the case with intuition. Again, how does intelligence function ? Or even what is intelligence ? When an action is taking place in the brain, when an animal is working on instinct, when a philosopher is working on intuition, when some brain is working either for intuitive perception or for intellectual reasoning, the actual processes involved in all these actions are not so well understood as to justify a differentiation between religion and science on such criteria. Hence the difference between science and religion on the basis of intelligence and intuition has no real validity.

Thus on the whole there is no basic difference between a scientist, a philosopher and a religious seer; only they generally practice on different planes on the same parameter. If we examine the function of science in general, we find that the scientist only perceives and records the pattern of events; the causal relationship between various events is beyond the scope of a scientist. The scientist does not, in fact cannot, study the causes of various relationships; he merely describes the beautiful pattern existing between different phenomena. For example, take the case of electricity. What does a scientist know about it ! What Faraday did was to discover that if certain materials are brought together in a certain relationship then some sort of current is generated which can be used for many purposes. In short, he said that if you do this then that will happen. The discovery of electricity is considered to be one of the greatest achievements of modern science but is this discovery not merely the description of certain phenomenon as it occurs ? It describes the pattern but does not explain it. Why do certain materials in a particular set-up give rise to the electrical current ? Or, to put the same question in a different field, why is sugar sweet ?

Why is salt saltish ? You cannot say that sugar is sweet because it contains succrose or that chilli is bitter because it contains a particular chemical. It is begging the question. To be dissatisfied with this sort of begging the question is to become a philosopher. It is the philosopher's problem to worry about such a why about things. It is for the philosopher to bother himself about the reason for the saltiness of the salt or sweetness of sugar. Science is not able to go beyond the obvious and that does not really solve the problem. Except that physics describes the pattern and chemistry describes the properties, science is unable to explain the fundamental problems of life. What science does is to see and observe but the reality remains unknown. Consequently, the more you as a scientist know, the more you become aware about the unknown, and the more you wonder about the unknown the more inspired you become. This is the transition from science to religion. How much are we filled with wonder and appreciation of Nature when we know that our galaxy is one of the myriads of galaxies ? How much are we filled with wonder as a result of the discoveries made with the help of microscope and telescopes, as a result of artificial satellites ? With every scientific discovery the sphere of the unknown assumes a stupendous magnitude. The field of the unknown is an expanding field. It expands much faster than the field of knowledge. Thus the field of religion is not restricted but expands with the expansion of science; the significance of religion is never limited by the expanding frontiers of science. Thus apart from the fact that science and philosophy are complementary in pursuit of Truth—one describes the pattern and the other tries to explain it—there is a very close relationship between science and religion. In fact, science leads to religion.

Arthur Eddington, James Jeans, Albert Einstein who rose to the highest positions through the ladder of science died in more religious frame of mind than many religious leaders. As a result of the deep study of the philosophical implications of their scientific researches they struck a note that the vast realm of the unknown is not only unknown but also unknowable. All the great scientists bow down to the unknowable and that constitutes the primary basis of relgion. Thus, the more high you go in science the more religious you can become. The more the scientists gain knowledge about the expanding universe the more they are filled with wonder and appreciation about the universe and the more religious they become.

Let us, for example, consider how life come into being. How did the animate originate from the inanimate ? This is one of the most fundamental problems about which even the religious thinkers have no satisfactory answer. Again, there are concepts like electricity, magnetism, energy, force, which are very important for the scientists but their ultimate nature remains mysterious. If you take the definition of Soul or even that of the Highest as found in the religious scriptures and the definition of energy as given by scientist and you take out the caption from the two then it will be difficult to say which was the definition of Soul and which was the definition of energy. Whether we consider the frontiers of science or that of religion we find that the circle of knowledge is situated within the circle of the Unknown. The mysteries of neither have been completely revealed.

Religion will not get a blow as a result of scientific advancement. There is no difference between the two. There is only a time-lag between the conclusions of science and the tenets of religion Take for example the Vedas which are some of the most ancient religious scriptures of the world. Let a reviewer compare them with a modern book of knowledge or encyclopaedia and he will be struck by a striking similarity in the content of the two. Obviously, the thinkers of the past whom we remember today as religious sages busied themselves in pursuits not essentially very much different from those of the modern thinkers in the fields of both science and philosophy. In fundamental principle, science and religion differ only in terminology. In practice, the two are complementary with a time-lag in between. Our religion of today cannot be but the result of the science of our ancient forefathers. It is but proper that the words *Veda* and *Science* both have their roots in the terms meaning *knowledge*.

THE SCIENCE OF NON-PHYSICAL NATURE

By
PROFESSOR J. B. RHINE
The Parapsychology Laboratory, Duke University, Durham, North Carolina, U.S.A.

Out of his sensory experience and the rational derivatives man has developed a general concept known as the physical universe. And out of the relationships that have been found to exist within this observed and inferred universe have emerged the recognised physical sciences and the physical bases of the other sciences. While from time to time there have been offerred hypotheses of non-physical factors in living organisms none of these has ever become orthodox, either in biology or psychology. There are, therefore, no conventionally recognized nonphysical operations in the natural world, and, according to prevailing thought, any occurrence not fundamentally reduciable to physical process would have either to be ignored or classed as supernatural (though such a category, too, is unacceptable in the sciences). Thus, even, though many individual scientists have reservations on the point, nature has in the sciences come to be effectively synonymous with the physical universe.

There has been only one small branch of inquiry to make a scientific attack on the question of non-phycial causation in nature. This branch of inquiry logically is a division of psychological study and is known today as *parapsychology* (and by various other names such as psychical research, metapsychics, psychic science, etc.). Its problem-domain includes those natural occurrences (now called *psi* phenomena) which do not submit to classification as physcical events. In more descriptive terms, parapsychology deals with the experiences and behaviour of living organisms that fail to show regular relationships with time, space mass, and other criteria of physicality.

Parapsychology began with the study of spontaneous psi (or psychic) experiences such as are fairly common throughout the world. These experiences appear to defy interpretation in terms of conventional principles. The more familiar of these were of cognitive nature, instances in which information was supplied to the person concerned, knowledge which he could not have acquired by way of the recognized sensory and rational channels. There were in such cases no adequate intermediating physical stimuli for interception by the sense organs. These spontaneous experiences, which had been familiar throughout the history of mankind, came to be identified as instances of *telepathy* if they seemed to involve a transfer of thought or feeling from one person to another, and *clairvoyance* if there appeared to be an awareness of an objective event not present to the senses.

Such occurrences became of special interest during the latter half of the nineteenth century when the pressure of mechanistic thinking deriving from the rapid advancement of the physical sciences challenged the spiritual concept of man. An effort was made at first to collect and study the spontaneous experiences themselves, as an evidence of extrasensory mode of perception, but this attempt gave way in time to experimental research into the problems suggested. Early experiments based on these claims of extrasensory perception (ESP) were generally exploratory in character. They did not, as was eventually recognized, distinguish adequately between the two forms, telepathy and clairvoyance. Naturally, there was to begin with no very clear concept of the basic characteristics of parapsychological phenomena; that is, what common features would identify them. The field had not yet acquired general outlines. But these exploratory tests sustained interest and stimulated further research. Criticism and discussion followed and led in time to the refinement of the test procedures.

By the second quarter of the present century, however, the development of methods had produced a crucial order of tests for extrasensory perception. The occurrence of ESP had, by the mid-thirties, been tested under conditions that even today, have not been seriously questioned. In the most definitive experiment conducted upto that time the best subject tested for ESP was able to identify the order of cards from shuffled packs located in another building, from 100 to 250 yards away, with a success of approximately 30% in a series of 1850 trials, tests in which the expectation on a theory of chance was but 20%. Since the theoretical probability of so great a result in such a series was of the order of 10^{-24}, it may be assumed that an effective relationship between subject and object had been demonstrated. In view of the distance involved and also other precautions against sensory cues only an extrasensory mode of perception could have produced the results. With recurrent patterning from one pack of cards to the other eliminated, both by shuffling and by the use of several decks of cards, rational inference on the part of the subject could not be considered as a reasonable alternative to ESP. With the provisions for independent recording (in duplicate) and even double surveillance during one section of the experiment, the hypothesis of error, whether deliberate or unconscious, was rendered improbable.

In the twenty years that have followed publication of these data many other series of experiments have been made by other investigators in the same and in other laboratories, some of them with even more elaborate precautions and more extensive design than the work described. Researches have also been conducted to distinguish between the types of ESP known as telepathy and clairvoyance. Both types of effects have been experimentally demonstrated, although in the case of telepathy it is not possible to say what the fundamental nature of the sender's operation is that constitutes the target. The mystery of the essential thought-brain relation for the present limits the investigation of the question of telepathy beyond this point.

If, as most serious scientific students who have followed the research developments will readily concede, the occurrence of ESP has been established, it will be allowable now to proceed to consider its challenge to physical explanation. In other words, assuming that extrasensory perception occurs, we may ask if it is extraphysical.

The very spontaneous experiences from which the experiments took their clue offered a challenge to physics in the first place. One of the most obvious features of these experiences is that two persons are as likely to have a telepathic experience when they are separated by thousands of miles as they are when only a short distance apart. In spontaneous experiences of clairvoyance, too, the distance scene is as likely to be perceived as that which is nearby. Moreover, a number of the exploratory tests of ESP, prior to the one described above, had involved considerable distances measured in miles, some of them even comparisons of different distances. The results failed to suggest any relationship of success in ESP to the proximity of the subject to the object.

The subject participating in the distance experiment mentioned above, in which 30% success was obtained at 100 to 250 yards, had, over a long series of previous tests, averaged approximately 32% successes with the target cards within a few feet of him. There was nothing, therefore, in the test results to indicate any lawful relationship whatever between distance and scoring rate. In the other experiments that involve distance, while it cannot be said that a nicely designed study, exhausting all possibilities, has ever yet been made the results have been the same—there is no reliable relation indicated.

No hypothesis of a physical relationship in ESP has ever arisen from the research results. The spontaneous cases had given no suggestion of any effect of distance and the experimental evidence confirmed the impression. And yet, as a matter of course, there have been many types of conditions from which such an hypothesis could have emerged had the evidence suggested it. There have been many different barriers imposed incidentally in the experimental conditions, barriers such as walls, buildings, mountains, and thousands of miles of atmosphere. Also, the target objects have been presented at various angles. In most cases these objects were cards. They have been located in various positions, in some instances with the back of the card toward the subject, in other cases in such a position that only an edge would be turned in the direction of the subject. In addition, for any theory of radiation there is the difficulty of discrimination between numerous objects in close proximity. For example, in many ESP tests the problem involves the attempt to identify cards packed in a box in which all twentyfive are less than a quarter of an inch thick. This proximity would obviously become a limiting condition for a physical hypothesis. But in spite of all the varieties of physical conditions under which ESP tests have been conducted, the results have consistently been such that no hypothesis of a physical relationship has been suggested.

One of the most striking features of the spontaneous experiences of ESP is the fact that they are almost as likely to involve future events as contemporaneous ones. A dream of disaster occurring to a loved one may precede the tragic event itself or may merely precede the arrival of the news coming from the scene which may be half way around the world. This suggestion that precognitive ESP might occur was reduced to experimental test following the definitive stage of ESP experiments mentioned above and so far as experimental comparisons have gone, the same relationship has been found as in the spontaneous cases; that is to say, time has not been found to be a limiting condition in the functioning of ESP. It is no handicap to ESP to be directed toward a target order of cards that is to be set up at a designated future time, as compared with a present order. This experimental result follows logically enough, not only from the spontaneous psi experiments but also from the results of the distance tests; it would be difficult to conceive of time as limiting a function that is independent of space. At least it will be difficult until science discovers an instance of time change involving no spatial change.

It would be too large an undertaking to recount here the steps through which the methods for testing precognitive ESP have progressed or to appraise the adequacy of the experimental design to meet the alternative hypotheses. As is natural in unfinished investigation, there still are those who have different degrees of confidence in the adequacy of the experiments thus far completed to establish a conclusive case for precognition. If, as now appears to many to be a reasonable conclusion, the case for precognitive ESP *has* been established, it will not be disputed that it is a radical development for psychology and for science in general. It introduces either an alternative to causation or a mode of causation independent of the time order.

*　　　*　　　*

Recoiling, however, as it naturally does from concepts it was more or less trained to reject, the educated mind demands a more developed rationale than mere statistical data on such a question as the actuality of ESP. This attitude has been frankly expressed by a number of scientific men. It is now happily possible to go far toward meeting this very human requirement and to offer a rationally cemented foundation of fact that is moderately extensive.

I have already referred to the consistency with which the various types of psi investigations have shown the same lack of a regular relation to physical conditions. This consistency extends into all the various areas of the research field, and these are too extensive to be effectively handled in a paper of this length.

Another of the tests of this lawfulness is the fact that it has been possible to use the standard scientific approach of hypothesis, prediction, and experimental verification to investigate psi. For example, on the strength of the distance tests of ESP it was possible to predict the results of the precognition tests. Again, it was inferred that if the law of reaction applied in ESP there should be some reaction upon the subject (e. g. the card) when a cognitive perception of it occurred to the subject. This led to the designing of delicate tests of the direct influence of the subject upon the object, tests of psychokinesis (PK) based on the throwing of dice. After about 20 years of investigation the position may safely be taken that such a direct psychokinetic effect has been demonstrated and independently confirmed.

The overall relationship of these operations between subject and object, with ESP on the cognitive side and PK on the kinetic, indicates a reversible psychophysical interaction between subject and object, one that does not involve the sensorimotor system of the individual. In ESP the essential similarities observed between the conditions affecting telepathy, clairvoyance, and precognition seem to indicate that the various forms of ESP atleast go back to one common perceptual function.

As psychological information concerning these various ESP effects accumulates it adds greatly to the rational understanding of the difficulties that have been encountered in the research. For example, when eventually it was recognized that psi is unconscious in all its types, it brought greater understanding of the puzzling effects encountered than had any other single discovery. Immediately the difficulties that had been found in controlling the capacity were more understandable. The peculiar experimental effects obtained, of which there had been many, fell at once into a more reasonable relationship. There was, for example, the well-known fact that sometimes a subject would score consistently below the chance average. This was for long a baffling occurrence, but psychologically such a performance on an unconscious level became understandable enough. The regular decline in the scoring rate which the subject had been found to show as he proceeded through his test run or other unit was at least partially clarified by the recognition of the unconsciousness of psi. Curious displacement effects and other distortions (preferential patterning, consistent missing, and the like) were no longer the puzzles they had been.

But the most recent extension of the rational network of psi relationships is that involving the investigation of psi in other animals, now that it has been established in man. Fifteen or more years ago the definite decision was taken to push the search for personality correlates of psi capacity. Surely, it was argued, some people have more of it than others. Quick identification of high scoring subjects would revolutionize the investigation of the elusive capacity. A wide range of selective methods were utilized and much seining and sifting was done. Differences in performance were actually found and some significant correlations obtained, but more and more as the studies progressed it became apparent that the results were not revealing a tie-up of the extent of native psi capacity with the trait measured; in stead,a relation to the more superficial quality of adaptability to the test situation was being demonstrated. Some of these correlates associated with scoring rate were even of transient nature as, for example, the subject's attitude of belief or scepticism toward ESP.

All this investigation was important; for one thing, it provided still more evidence of the occurrence of psi. But it was not leading the investigator to any group of subjects that had a monopoly on psi capacity or even a special amount of the gift. By the time the survey had extended to a considerable extent over the various classifications of abnormality and subnormality and into some of the racial subdivisions, it finally became evident that psi must be a capacity that, in evolutionary origin, antedated man himself. In order to check on this hypothesis it was necessary to look for psi in animals. Although this excursion into species other than man is a new and recent one, it has already brought up sufficient evidence to necessitate continuance and at least to permit the conclusion that man is, indeed, not the only species in possession of psi functions.

It is an important fact that two parallel lines of study are possible in parapsychology, based on the one hand on the comparative analysis of large collections of spontaneous psychic experiences rich in suggestions for investigation, and, on the other, the experimental findings of the Laboratory on which the conclusions are more definitely based. The opportunity for checking findings from one to the other in these two very different lines of empirical study provides a special advantage and an exceptional quality of reassurance. Very little has been found thus far by the one that has not also been encountered in the other except effects observed in the spontaneous material that cannot yet be brought to laboratory test.

And, finally, there are certain very general rational considerations that favour parapsychology as against the physicalistic philosophy that constitutes the main bar to its acceptance. First, as I have already stated, investigations of ESP arose from the need to explain actual reports of human experiences of types that have run persistently through all recorded cultures and that, essentially in the same patterns, still recur in our most sophisticated centres of human society today. No such basis in human experience can be claimed for any version of physicalism. Second, this concept of a non-physical function in personality runs as a fundamental belief throughout the history of the social institutions of man, most conspicuously those dealing with his religious life. The only culture remotely approximating a physicalistic philosophy of man is that of communism. Whatever rational support, then, may rightly be derived from the argument of long enduring social utility is against the philosophy that is opposed to psi.

While so brief a sketch of the growing rationale of the psi discoveries omits whole sections of data and relationships, it may serve to show that parapsychology at least is now past the point where its body of knowledge was composed of scattered, isolated, disconnected chunks of statistical findings. It now makes a great deal of sense.

* * *

It may more appropriately be the work of others than the parapsychologists to attempt larger rational setting for psi in the scheme of knowledge. Any suggestions of this setting that may be made by the investigator as he proceeds are, of course, subject to the most careful reviewing. But they may serve the purpose of stimulating discussion on points that might otherwise be allowed to go undeveloped. It is always safe, at least, to raise questions.

For example, is it not the part of wisdom to try to fit the psi functions as far as possible into the familiar concept of causation even though the serial order of cause-effect relations as known from the physical world would not apply to precognition. One knows at least where the difficulty of squarring the new with the old is localized in such an approach and in such a problem area one needs to take short and cautious steps.

Likewise, might not the same logic that has produced the concepts of the various energies involved in physical theory profitably be followed to the point of suggesting that a psi energy be hypothesized? It is true, there is not much use in setting up hypotheses unless they can be brought around to empirical test; but some initial thought is necessary to discover if this step is feasible.

It is no great jump from the broad concept of energy as it now prevails in physical theory over to the notion of a special state of energy that is not interceptible by any of the sense organs. Certain physical energies are already in that category. Psi energy would, of course, have to be a kind that does not regularly relate to time, space, and mass as do the better known forms of energy, but there is discussion among theoretical physicists of exceptions to this relationship in the operation of types of energies that are already recognized. For the most part physicists themselves do not balk at the notion of a state of energy operating out of the currently familiar framework of concepts. After all, the effects, the signs of "work being done", are there. It was for this that the concept of the energies were invented.

Whatever it may be that is causing these psi manifestations has naturally to be a convetrible sort of influence; for example, in PK the effect has to register in the motion of the target object (e.g. the falling die). In ESP the transition into consciousness whatever the nature of that operation is, and from consciousness into a verbal or manual response, involves more interconversions, changes that are still for the most part unsolved mysteries in both psychology and physiology. It adds little burden to the rational mind, therefore, to recognize that the energy of psi has to be convertible to other forms in order to be detected as an occurrence in nature.

It may be tentatively proposed, then, that back of the phenomena of psi must exist an energy that interoperates with and interconverts to those other energetic states already familiar to physics. Psi energy is imperceptible by the sense organs and does not in any way yet discovered regularly function within the framework of time and space and mass, and yet does lawfully operate with intelligent purpose within the personality of the organism, though on an unconscious level. It probably belongs to the early evolutionary equipment of the organism and represents a more primitive relation between the organism and the environment. Possibly it antedates the sensorimotor system (which, of course, interacts with known energy forms and produces specific modalities of perception and behaviour for the most part conscious, at least on man).

* * *

The key significance of the psi function lies, of course, in the fact that it can be measured and otherwise studied with respect to the criteria of physicality and demonstrated to depart from those criteria. Much of the rest of personality and the life functions of animals is, on this point, ambiguous and elusive and throughout the history of science has allowed completely opposite interpretations to prevail. Psi phenomena alone bring the issue into focus and allow a decision to be reached as to whether or not the organism possesses extraphysical powers. The investigation of psi has thus provided a scientific way of dealing with the question of the nature of man with respect to the physical world.

Without a reliable answer to this question of man's nature, it is not possible to solve intelligently the most important problems confronting mankind. To appreciate the importance of this issue of the bearing of physicalism on human life, it is necessary only to condsider the consequences of a strict application of a thoroughly mechanistic theory of man.

The most far-reaching and revolting consequence lies in what would happen to volitional or mental freedom. Under a mechanistic determinism the cherished voluntarism of the individual would be nothing but idle fancy. Without the exercise of some freedom from physical law, the concepts of character, responsibility, moral judgment and democracy would not survive critical analysis. The concept of a spiritual order, either in the individual or beyond him, would have no logical place whatever. In fact, little of the entire value system under which human society has developed would survive the establishment of a thoroughgoing philosophy and physicalism.

If the importance of the psi investigations is

of this general order, it is urgent then not to lose the essential focus upon its principal advantage, the method of inquiry itself. It is always and perhaps unavoidably the case that new inquiries tend to generate excessive disputation over terms, interpretations, and significances. In the psi researches reviewed above there is not enough either of essential novelty or of anything approaching finality to justify taking a strongly formulated stand and holding out for any important decision at this particular point. Rather, the merit lies in the possibilities opened up : Parapsychology has verified by relatively improved methods some old claims of powers that transcend the properties of material systems. How much more can be found out about the properties of these nonphysical operations ? What more can be done with and about them ? What kind of a universe must it be that combines them and the physical world ? One sees no end to questions, following one upon another. There is no time to lose over unessential issues and fruitless niceties.

One single well-established fact of parapsychology is enough to trigger such a programme. Over against the iron wall of physical determinism one unmistakable sign of another order of reality is enough to justify a full-scale inquiry, a concentrated compaign of investigation to see what kind of world there is that could produce such a manifestation. Traces and faint signs have time and again in the history of discovery betokened the presence of hidden systems of reality.

Science still "moves but slowly, slowly, creeping on from point to point" as it did in Tennyson's day. But those who are most familiar with the halting, handicapped way in which radical scientific advances have been made in the past will understand the difficulties and delays. They will appreciate, too, the timely challenge the psi researches make to a philosophy of man that, over most of the world, across national and even ideological boundaries, dominates the scientific thinking of today. Tomorrow that philosophy may, unless challenged and effectively refuted, curtain the entire range of thought for mankind everywhere.

SCIENCE, PHILOSOPHY AND RELIGION

By

DR. V. K. R. V. RAO

Member, Planning Commission

(Ex-Vice Chancellor, Delhi University)

Philosophy, as far as I know anything of it, is not afraid of dealing with truth, and there is nothing, therefore, that should stand in the way of religious minded people or even the Theosophical minded people from discussing the relationship between Religion, Philosophy and Science.

Let me take the subject in this way : What is religion ? What is its relation to philosophy, and what is the relationship of science to philosophy ? And ulitimately, we come to the final question, what is the relationship of science to religion ?

Religion is a word that means many things to many people. Some people identify religion with rituals. Some people identify it with practices of one kind or another; some people identify it with taboos and inhibitions and restraints of various kinds; others identify it with a particular way of life, a particular attitude towards human beings. Most of these people, however, identify religion with belief in God. Perhaps religion started with a sense of fear, but I do not think fear was the only or even the major motive.

I think the idea of God really came from a sense of awe and wonder.

Religion meant worship; and in worship you humble yourself. You, so to speak , admit your smallness. You admit your littleness before something much mightier, something much bigger than yourself. It is in a way the greatest antidote to egoism. The original human-beings were filled with a great sense of awe and wonder; and that is what God meant, in the first instance, something wonderful, something bigger, something that stimulated in oneself a feeling of beauty, of exaltation, and of great longing. It is true that one considered as God anything which was powerful, anything which was mysterious; anything which was lofty and magnificient became God, and you find this confirmed in the Tenth Chapter of the Gita, a Chapter which I am personally very fond of. In this chpater Arjuna asks the Lord Krishna to describe Himself. Arjuna says, 'You are God. Nobody knows you better than yourself. Will you tell me something about yourself !' It is a most wonderful chapter. There you will find that the Lord describes Himself in analogies : 'I am Meru of high mountains, of immovable things the Himalayas, of streams the Ganga am I, of lakes I am the ocean, and among the seasons I am spring.' Therefore, the biggest, the tallest, the noblest of everything became identified with God.

There was an element of unexplainability in God. Apart from anything else, one of the element of God was unexplainability, something you could not understand, something you could not explain. Therefore, there was awe and wonder, and there was surrender. It is in that sense that you find an antithesis between religion and science because in religion the kind of thing that developed was something which could not be explained. There was something you could not explain, and when you could not explain it, it became God. Anything that you could not understand, you could not find the reason for became God, and this is the major thing that became religion. I do not say this is the only attribute of religion, but it was built on inability to understand phenomena, or to control it. Thus things which he could not understand, things which overpowered him by their might, or by their magnificence, man called gods, the morning sun became the Sun God—and you gave them a divine place. That is to say, divinity was mixed with all sorts of things, things which you could not understand, things which were magnificent, things which were beautiful, things which were grand and so on.

From that developed a religious outlook which tended to explain things, not explain them properly, but which tended to say, 'Oh, yes, this happened because it is a divine phenomenon; this is a work of God; this is a work of Indra, this is a work of Vayu or Vamana, or this is the work of some other god.' And therefore, if you want to bend a particular phenomenon into your own requirements, you had to worship, you had to perform *yajna*, you had to perform sacrifices, you had to sing, dance and paint, you had to do all sorts of things. That is to say, the conquest of nature was to be brought about, not by understanding the secrets of its working but by praising God, by worshipping Him and asking Him to come and help you out of a particular situation. As for example, even today, a large number of people would turn to worship for the solution of their problems, which many others would regard as problems which should be dealt with in a different way altogether. That is, so to speak, there is at the one end what you may call religion, one aspect of religion, undoubtedly not the whole of religion, and at the other end there is the scientific outlook.

I feel there is no doubt that the religious outlook has very much developed in this country. There is no doubt that in India many things are explained in the name of gods and goddesses. As a matter of fact, on gods and goddesses much more things are thrust in this country than they really deserve, almost anything which one does not understand, which one needs to get or wants to avoid. This attitude really springs out of the feeling of awe and the feeling of fear.

Then you have, as against that religious outlook, at the other end of the scale, the scientific outlook. The scientist says that every phenomenon has a cause. Everything has a cause; if it rains there is a cause; if it is hot there is a cause; if it is not hot then also there is a cause; if an individual gets cholera or small-pox there is a cause; if he dies there is a cause; if he does not die there is a cause; there is nothing, therefore, without a cause. Mountains can be climbed, oceans can be crossed, sky can be reached. There are planets and you can travel to them. Five years ago people would not have dreamt of it but now people are planning a time table of inter-planetary travel. The scientific outlook is based on two things : there is supreme confidence in the human intellect, and on the other hand, a mystical belief that everyhing in the world can be explained. I say mystical belief because nobody knows if that belief is cent per cent sound or not. The scientists believe that everything in the world can be explained; every phenomenon can be explained and understood. If you cannot explain, you have not found the reason but the reason is there. Religion also has something of that confidence but without subject to any kind of test. The scientific outlook implies the belief that everything can be explained and allied with that is the supreme confidence in the human capacity to explain things. That is the direct antithesis of the religious outlook where one says that certain things cannot be explained because they are divine and are the work of gods and goddesses or of one God. Therefore, all that you should do is to feel awed and to ask for mercy, ask for succour.

Science explained in this way and religion in the sense in which we have explained now are therefore, so to speak, at opposite ends of the scale. And Philosophy is the bridge that links science and religion, that gives to science what is its due and tries to show that there is no antithesis, in the last analysis, between the two—Science and Religion.

What is Philosophy ? Why do we claim this particular task or this particular function to Philosophy ?

Philosophy, in a way, is nothing but the application of the scientific outlook to the problems of man's relationship to the supernatural, with the awe which he feels for the supreme things and with the complications resulting from his environment and so on. Science seeks to ask questions, tries to find reasons and ventures to give explanations. Not that science does not admit being impressed by grandeur, beauty, and the like, but its primary role is to seek knowledge and therefore to ask questions why is this, why is that, why is suffering, why do people die, why do young become old, why do old ones die. Why are people born ? Asking these questions, trying to find out an answer and not just accept an answer based on authority even if it were enunciated by Prophets or by religion, that is a scientific process, it is quest for truth.

What is scientific outlook ? What is scientific method ? In fact, it is an application of logic, it is an attempt to find out mutual consistency or mutual contradiction. The whole of philosophy was really nothing but the application of intellect to religion, while religion is in the last analysis not based on intellect. Religion has its roots in a kind of mystic feeling in human beings which makes us feel that in the world of phenomena there is something grand, something large, and yet there is no dispute about the genuineness of this feeling. From time to time you get this feeling that there is something bigger than all the world you have seen. Now, that kind of mystical feeling is a sort of intuitive perception, which is not based on logic, verification, and experimentation but that is a kind of mystery.

Then, you have philosophy which is an application of logic, application of the scientific method, application of the mind to the problems of existence, the problems of life and death, to the problems of human sufferings and the problems of God and religion itself. Now, while the advance of science is likely to eliminate or weaken religion in its 'primitive' sense of superstition, ritual and strange practices—the aspect of religion where you make gods and goddesses out of phenomena in nature when you do not explain them, when you cannot understand them, when you cannot conquer a phenomenon in nature and it becomes a god or goddess—, undoubtedly such things will get corroded with the advance of science; but I am convinced that science will not destroy religion in India. In fact, science will explain phenomena which could not be understood before. Science explains, understands and conquers; with the help of science you can climb to the top of the Himalayas without the least difficulty. Even without climbing over it you can fly over it if you have an appropriate plane and you have no trouble at all. Science conquers underground, overground, super-space, lower space, under the sea and occeans and under the ice. You have heard all about sputniks, satellite planets and man-made artificial planet. When science understands, explains and conquers, it is bound to take away that part of religion which is based on inability to understand and inability to conquer.

When you conquer fire and understand fire, the god of fire disappears as *Agni* God. It is no longer unexplained, then how can it be God ? God is not somebody whom you can ride on by power. If He is the embodiment of a phenomenon which is understood by your intellect, He is not God any more, it is fancy; it is something fanciful. So the Sun God, the Rain God, the God of Fire, the God of Wind, Mountains and Forests, one by one melt away because of the warmth and heat and light produced by science. Does anything then remain ? When a phenomenon is understood, expalined and conquered, it is no longer mysterious, awe-inspiring, and something fearful, but still there remains a philosophy, an understanding of the various relationships. Even when everything is explained, philosophy remains there.

Philosophy can be religious, it may not be religious. You have got philosophy which is religious and which is not religious, which admits the existence of God and which denies the existence of God. You have certain philosophy which asks for special attitude to life which believes in nature, in ethos, but does not believe in God. On the other hand, there is another philosophy which does not only believe in ethos, in special attitude, conduct of duty, but also believes in God as the foundation of all activities, of all beauty, and then you have got the most mystical, the most wonderful attempt such as the world has ever seen and I do not think it can ever see again which is made in the Bhagavad Gita, which is to identify all things, identify knowledge and work and worship, make them alternative ways and yet identical. Again, you have the concept of God which is beyond all activities, which is beyond all the various things which means reality to us, which is, therefore, really beyond reality. That is philosophy.

Philosophers are all logicians. The philosopher is necessarily a logician. He is not a poet. A philosopher is always a person who applies logic and is always drawing inferences, destroying contradictions and going from step to step exactly the way a scientist proceeds with the crucial difference that the scientist has got experimentation, prediction and verification, if his prediction comes right, he is right. He can experiment, he can isolate. He is, therefore, much more advantageously placed in the quest of truth than the philosopher who has only got his mind and the laws of logic to go after truth. Though in this great country of ours, we have also had, over and above philosophers, the 'men of God', the persons who experiment in the discovery of God, which is pure mysticism.

In this country you have had from time to time human beings who experiment upon themselves, who seek to discover God, rather what they call God, and they have done so with confidence. They have made assertions that they have seen God, that they know God, and they inspire confidence in the veracity of their experience. No country in the world is richer in 'men of God' than this country. Within our living memory or in quite recent history, we have had such men, as Shri Ramkrishna Paramhansa, Shri Aurobindo, Shri Ramana Maharshi and others, who identified themselves with the Supreme and realized God face to face in modern times, not in the days of the Vedas, the Mahabharata and the Ramayana. How do you identify a 'man of God'? How do you identify the man who has discovered God and identified himself with the Supreme? He is known by the complete harmony and peace he has attained, by the complete indifference to the normal things that matter from our point of view. He is recognized by the way he is able to stimulate the higher self in the people who come into contact with him and the sense of peace and harmony that he is able to pass on to them even though only temporarily.

Now, what is the relationship between these and religion? What is that religion? Of course, it is too vast a subject and I am too small a person to talk about it, I do not have courage to talk to you in any confident terms about religion in the big sense, but what does religion indicate? It does not rest on lack of explanation; it does not rest on lack of understanding; it rests on what one may call understanding based on perception within oneself. It does not involve lack of logic, does not involve rituals, does not involve sacrifices, it does not involve superstition, and yet, it does proclaim that behind all this phenomenon, all this power, conquest of nature beyond all these, there is some Reality, which the sages and seers have realized and proclaimed as God, and that only nature and environment do not constitute Reality. While nature and environment constitute a part of reality, there is a Reality which is different from these, which is so to speak, reality from within. There is a reality from within, which is much more real than any phenomenon that you find in the environment.

Now, that Reality people define in various ways. They describe it in various fashions : Conscience, Soul, *Atma*, *Purushottama*, and so on and so forth, but probably, nobody knows it. But your not-knowing does not make you unscientific. It is not the same kind of not-knowing which led you to discover a God in a mountain; in a torrent or in a lightning, thunder or storm. Here it is not non-understanding, rather here it is based on a conception that there are people who have understood. Ultimately, you know that in this country people have discovered God scientifically, but to be in a position to discover God, you have got to be very special. You and I cannot be Einstein; if you want to be Einstein, you have got to be extra-special. You and I cannot discover another planet; we may be professors but in order to be a man of science, who has discovered wonders of science you have got to be extra-special. Nobody knows wherefrom that extra-special comes.

Science has advanced a great deal; by cutting a particular nerve you destroy memory, you can destory reflexes. All sorts of advances are taking place in the knowledge of the human body, in the knowledge of mind and brain, yet nobody knows wherefrom this inner consciousness comes. This inner consciousness, which is described in one of the chapters of the Bhagvad Gita in terms of *Sakshi* is ever a witness within you. Not all the time, but occasionally you become conscious of it, nonetheless, it remains there witnessing all you do, all the time. If you identify yourself with this *Sakshi* you will be different. It is possible for the smallest of us, the lowest of us, occasionally to get a glimpse of it, something which is apart from oneself, which stands up, which watches with amusement as one goes about doing the different things that one is doing. Occasionally, one gets a feeling of surprise: 'What is it that I. am doing? What is it all about?'

Therefore, as far as India is concerned, religion is not just based on faith; it is based on the fact that men who have discovered God come and tell us that they have discovered so. It has some relationship to the method of science in so far as men who proclaimed their belief in God are men who have experimented with themselves, who have tried themselves and who affirm that knowledge on the basis of their own experience. Whether it is in the Punjab or Bengal, in Tamilnad or in Maharasthra, in Uttar Pradesh or in Rajasthan, this country is full of men and women who claim that they have seen God, that they have experienced God and that they have become conscious of God. This really means that they have become conscious of something within themselves which is different from the bundle of complexes and reactions which constitute a normal human being. Therefore, I would say that the march of science, so far as India is concerned, should not lead to the destruction of religion. It may lead to the destruction of superstitions and rituals but it would not lead to the destruction of religion in terms of One Universal Life. With that consciousness of the universal identity, with that consciousness of something—call it Soul, call it Spirit, call it anything you like, but that exists in you, in me, in the environment, in the mountains, in the stars, in rivers, the fire, in the moving and the unmoving, in everything—with this experience of the universal consciousness, universal spirit, the march of science need not lead to disbelief in religion.

I have spoken largely out of ignorance, and you will forgive me if I have been talking nonsense. I regard myself scientific minded, but that does not prevent me from being religious minded at the same time.

BORDERLINE BETWEEN SCIENCE, PHILOSOPHY & RELIGION

By

PROF. T. R. SESHADRI, F.R.S.

Head of the Chemistry Department, Delhi University

I am glad to meet persons belonging to this group, because they are interested in what we call higher life. According to Shri Shankaracharya there are three things extremely rare in this world; these are human birth, the longing for liberation and the protecting care of a perfected sage. If one gets this rare human body, what is it fit for ? It is eminently fit for gaining liberation, and that is why later on, he goes on to say that if this wonderful human body, which is the best instrument for gaining liberation, is not used to achieve this end, but used for other purposes, there can be no greater suicide. Examining this point further, is the human body well fitted for other purposes, for example for full enjoyment of food ? If we eat too much, we get into difficulty, or if we eat rich food, we also get into trouble. Pigs do not seem to get into trouble at all, no matter how much they eat and enjoy. By such analysis we eventually come to the inevitable conclusion that the best that one could get out of this human body is liberation, a higher life, something much richer than what an animal can achieve.

Now let us examine the subject, viz, Borderline between Science, Philosophy and Religion. First we have to know what Science is, what Philosophy is and what Religion is ? Have they got any contacts ? Is there any borderline ? The common knowledge is that they are different things in life and have no borderline. Some may say that they are not different, and they are the same, only with different names. These names are intended only to create artificial barriers, and differences, and then to speak of borderlines.

Science has been defined in different ways; there can be a narrow definition, and there can be an all embracing definition. Some consider that science is knowledge and includes the methods of acquiring knowledge and using it. If we accept a wide definition like that, everything goes into science. Then, there is no separate item, called philosophy or religion; all came under science. But in common parlance we usually consider that science is concerned with knowledge of things outside us, the dividing line being our body. It may be more correct to say that science pertains to knowledge of the physical world.

We have been progressing rapidly in scientific knowledge. We have gained more extensive knowledge and also more intensive knowledge. Both ways there has been great progress. We could take as an example our knowledge of the earth, the sun and the stars; geography and astronomy have grown big. We can now see things farther and farther off. There were days not very long back, when the earth was considered to be a flat disc. There was fear in the minds of sailors sailing farther and farther out into the ocean that in the night they would just drop down from the disc and go down, they did not know where, into abysmal depths. Even the explanation of how the sun rises everyday in the east was based on this idea. It was believed that when we all sleep during the night, he goes around the horizon, behind the mountains and comes back again to the east. This served as an explanation and people were satisfied with it. Then came more knowledge and it was realised that the earth was not a disc, and it is round, and that the earth was not the centre of the universe, but the sun was the centre of this solar system and the earth went round it. In fact there are infinite numbers of stellar systems. We now feel that the universe is expanding at unimaginably great speed and we do not know how far it will expand. New items of knowledge are coming as we study the subject more and more; for example, some think that new matter is being created.

We shall now take an example more subtle. It belongs to the field of chemistry and is not so easily appreciated. Let us take the case of a crystal of sugar. The common man sees that it is beautiful, colourless and sparkling. It is edible and sweet and many good things can be made out of it. For nearly a hundred years many scientists have been trying to understand its secrets and explain why it is beautiful, soluble and sweet.

The crystal is built up of innumerable small molecules arranged in an orderly manner. Its composition was determined by a method invented by Liebig and it was found that each molecule contained 45 atoms; 12 carbon atoms, 22 hydrogen atoms and 11 oxygen atoms. More work showed that they are arranged in clusters or groups containing carbon, hydrogen and oxygen atoms. These are present in the form of two rings with an oxygen bridge between them. The rings are not planar; they are three dimensional and look like chairs. Some groups are linked vertical to the plane of the rings and some horizontal. The picture has become more and more complex and more and more clear. The molecules are not static, but extremely dynamic. They breathe in and out and the various groups oscillate. In a crystal free motion is restricted. However, in the gaseous state and in solution the molecules move about and rotate. This does not take into consideration the inner details of the 45 atoms present in the sugar molecule. Each has its own structure and resembles the solar system; each has a planetary system of electrons and has a heavy nucleus consisting of protons and neutrons. All this detail or complexity exists in a tiny molecule of sugar and millions of these molecules make up the crystal. In a small compass it is a universe comparable to that of astronomy.

Having given these examples, I wish to mention that there are two important methods by which knowledge is obtained and developed. The first is the experimental method in which data are collected and conclusions are arrived at. There are various methods of making observations. Looking through instruments like the microscope, telescope or spectroscope is easily understood. But there are complex methods used in chemical study; colour reactions, generation of heat, change in physical properties are all employed. Besides this experimental method, there is the theoretical method based on the application of certain fundamental laws. It has been said that the falling of an apple revealed to Newton the existence of the Law of Gravitation and he applied it to the study of celestial bodies. There are other similar laws such as those of Thermodynamics and Quantum Theory which pertain to energy changes. The phenomena of chemical combinations and decompositions have been exciting a great deal of interest and study. Why does oxygen and hydrogen combine together to form water ? How do many other changes take place, changes that are vital to arts and industries and also those related to biological growth and decay ? Earlier a Swedish chemist, Berzelius gave a simple explanation based on the electrical nature of the elements. This was later found to be inadequate and explanations based on the electrons are now used. The development of the Theory of Resonance and of Wave Mechanics have provided clearer pictures. The two methods of approach, experimental and theoretical, are complementary to each other and one is used to verify the other. However, correct observation and experience provide the final decision in science.

Let us now turn to philosophy. There was a time, not long ago when philosophy was better known and science was still young and was called experimental philosophy or natural philosophy. This probably expresses the distinction adequately. If science belongs to the physical world, philosophy pertains to the subtler aspects of life and human endeavour. It may be said to deal with intangibles or with the inner life of beings. The subject is naturally more difficult and the chances of going wrong are therefore greater. I had once a discussion on this subject with an eminent Professor of Philosophy. According to him there are three kinds of philosophy. The first is of course the true one, 'True Philosophy' which is based on correct experience and verification and on sound reason. In its methods, it is the same as science except that it deals with different theme. The second kind is the 'Arm-chair philosophy'. It is one of convenience and takes the path of ease, shutting its eyes to contradictory facts and experience. The third is the 'Asura Philosophy' which perverts and confuses. For the common man and even for learned men it is difficult to distinguish between them, because of the subtle nature of philosophy and the intangible things it deals with. Verification is beset with serious difficulties. However, one thing seems to be clear that true philosophy is very close to true science. They are not mutually exclusive; they are in fact complementary.

We could now spend a few minutes on thinking of what I consider to be religion. There are many ideas of religion. Many think that temple worship is religion and many others may think that charity and service to Humanity is religion.

I take my definition of religion from the great authority of Swami Vivekananda. His definition is as follows : "Each soul is potentially divine. The Goal is to manifest this divine within, by controlling Nature, external and internal. Do this either by work, or worship, or psychic control, or philosophy, by one, or more, or all of these—and be free. This is the whole of religion. Doctrines or dogmas, or rituals, or books, or temples, or forms, are but secondary details". Now if we take this definition of religion, there is very little difficulty in reconciling science, philosophy and religion. The borderline is something we have for the sake of convenience put down, but in fact, science leads to philosophy and philosophy to religion. Actually the theoretical aspect of science is really the philosophical aspect. Well then, science deals with nature without and philosophy deals with nature within us, and religion deals with the manifestation of Divinity by controlling nature within and without.

I may mention here another important point. It has been the ambition of all workers in science and philosophy to know the Ultimate. What is the purpose of discovering laws ? If we discover the laws of Nature we get deeper insight into the workings of Nature and can understand the details easily. I shall give you an example from chemistry. A great Russian Chemist, Mendeleef discovered the law of Periodic Classification according to which the 92 elements of Nature are arranged in the form of a table which reveals the behaviour of the elements. The discoverer of freon, the gas so conveniently and safely used in refrigerators, got his inspiration from this Periodic Law. He gave the title of his Perkin Medal Address as 'From Periodic Classification to Production'. The key of knowledge was the Periodic Classification, and using that key he made his discovery. In science therefore the goal has been to discover the fundamental laws, to know the ultimate, and to know that by knowing which all others become known. That is also the purpose of philosophy and religion and that unites them all together. In fact they are essentially one, and are best considered to be different sides of the same coin.

SCIENCE AND THE GANDHIAN THOUGHT

By

ACHARYA SHRIMAN NARAYAN

Member, Planning Commission, New Delhi

It is useful to talk of the Gandhian Thought from the point of view of science, because Mahatma Gandhi was essentially a rational person, who had scientific approach to every problem of life. Sometimes it is felt in our country as well as in many others that Gandhiji was a sentimental person who believed in some kind of Utopia, which was far removed from modern science. I had the privilege of being in close touch with Gandhiji for a number of years. We had many opportunities of discussing many problems together, a number of economic, social, educational and political questions, and I was impressed by his deeply rational and scientific outlook. I felt attracted to his ideas primarily because his thoughts were rational and practical, not theoretical and visionary. I would, therefore, place before you some of his thoughts and try to show how they were scientific, not only when he talked about them, but even several decades ahead of his time.

Firstly, let us take up the question of non-violence. We are trying non-violence in every sphere. We talk of non-violence in the form of

Panchayats in political sphere, in the form of decentralization in social sphere. Is this non-violence a set of beliefs or a scientific theory ? If science has to be constructive and not to annihilate mankind, every weapon has to be non-violent. Take for example, the thermo-nuclear weapons and the atomic energy. This atomic energy can be used for destructive purposes, it can be used in a constructive way. There is an endless scope for its industrial uses. India is committed to the ideas of Gandhiji, which implies that the atomic power could be used only for peaceful purposes. Humanity can make tremendous progress with the peaceful uses of the atomic power. For example, agricultural production can be increased several fold with its help. The same is true of industries. The essence of the Gandhian approach towards such problems is that the scientific instruments should be used only for constructive goals. The world may desire to use this atomic power for destructive and evil purposes, but according to Gandhian thinking that would be the improper use of any natural energy.

Again, take the idea of village and small industries. Very often, people have questioned the necessity of having these industries after attaining our political freedom. To this, Gandhian answer is simple and categorical. Gandhiji had many discussions on this point and he always maintained that he was neither against machinery nor against any power being used in the country. But he had two conditions for the same. "My first condition", he said, "is that everybody must have work, and secondly, everybody must have work for eight hours a day". Mahatma Gandhi thought that the craze for labour-saving devices would take us nowhere and in a country like India such devices would create much unemployment. Even in America, which is always thinking of using them, there is huge unemployment. There are millions of people unemployed in that country as a result of the introduction of mechanical power. When population is small, the substitution of machines for human labour may be justified, but even then, its necessity has not been clearly demonstrated. In the United States of America, all unemployed persons are given doles and this is socially undesirable Imagine the condition when more that five million persons are getting about thousand rupees a month and have nothing to do. What a tremendous social waste and moral degradation ! That kind of thing, Gandhiji thought, will not only ruin the society, but will destroy the moral sense of the individual. Such a system will ruin India. That will be exploitation of the society, visibly or invisibly, whatever you may call it. The economists think that frictional unemployment is more or less inevitable in the modern economic system and it may roughly amount to three per cent of the total employment. In absolute magnitude, it amounts to a colossal figure. It involves millions of people in a country like India. Such technological devices which could create that amount of unemployment cannot be, according to Gandhiji, a scientific proposition.

In Russia and China, there is no mass unemployment, but in these countries, it is achieved as a result of military compulsions. In Russia, everybody is forced to work and to produce whatever he could. You cannot remain idle in a communist country, because it is thought that if you are idle, you are not producing any economic goods, and that is not possible under military controls. In some communist countries, for example in the U.S.S.R. if you are unable to produce anything, you will be given subsistence allowance. But that is so only when you are physically incapacitated, otherwise, work you must. Under the democratic set-up, the situation is different. You have freedom to work as well as to starve, but Gandhiji did not want either. He was opposed to the European system of democracy as well as the Russian system of totalitarianism. He wanted the system where *everybody* must work and earn his bread with his sweat.

The modern theory of economic development has emphasized that national planning without full employment is futile and meaningless. In under-developed countries full employment can be provided only through a wide-spread network of small and cottage industries. Introduction of technological improvements and electrical power with this objective is not ruled out. Acharya Vinoba Bhave, who is the greatest living exponent of the Gandhian thought, is prepared to use even atomic energy for a *charkha* and other small machines. But any machine or any power which de-humanizes man and compels him to unemployment and idleness cannot be considered rational at all. To Gandhiji, man was more important than machines.

According to Mahatma Gandhi, non-violence is the essence of social life. He advocated decentralization in political affairs in the form of *Panchayats* because he regarded a centralized administration as a store-house of violent potentialities. He pleaded for decentralization of industries because he looked upon large-scale and highly mechanized industries as the focal centres of social violence owing to the creation of mass unemployment. Gandhiji was essentially a practical idealist who looked at all problems from a realistic standpoint. He was convinced that modern science without non-violent outlook would precipitate global disaster.

It is not correct to say, as many persons do, that Gandhiji was behind his time. In fact, he was a practical visionary. Whether we considered social reforms, untouchability, family planning or prohibition, in every sphere Gandhiji went to the root of the matter. Take for example, prohibition. Gandhiji in this connection emphasized that the financial loss to the state exchequer due to the loss of excise duties should not be the main consideration of the government in deciding its policy regarding prohibition or any other such items, but the number of families ruined and degraded as a result of drinking or other such habits should also be taken into account. Prohibition directly helped such families and thus, augmented the social gain.

Mahatma Gandhi always emphasized that he did not want to establish any cult or any 'ism', but he was very clear about the role of science in human development and progress. He was not against technological innovations, but he depracated the social degradation resulting from them. Gandhiji himself conducted many experiments to improve the quality of *charkha*, which is also a kind of machine. What Mahatma Gandhi emphasized was the non-violent outlook in every sphere. In fact, he could be considered a non-violent scientist. To use a recent phrase of our Prime Minister, Mahatma Gandhi was a "Yogi Scientist", who desired to exploit science for the good of mankind. That is the only way for the salvation of humanity; there is no better way for the world of today.

SOME THOUGHTS ON UNIVERSAL LIFE

By

SHRI T. V. R. TATACHARI

Advocate, Supreme Court of India

The modern science is an ally of Divine Wisdom. Science is essentially concerned with the observation of facts as they exist in nature. The scientist observes these facts with his five senses. Sometimes mechanical instruments aid the scientists in their observations. These observations are recorded, classified and analyzed and then conclusions are drawn from them. The basis of scientific generalizations is the observation of facts. Religious philosophy is also the result of observation of facts in nature, but in this field of enquiry the observation is not only with the five senses. For it, certain other faculties which the human beings possess are also used. A student of physical science makes use of only his five known senses such as, touch, smell, sight, hearing and taste, whereas a student of Divine Wisdom makes use of other ways of acquiring knowledge also. These faculties are clairvoyance, clairaudience, telepathy and other faculties of psychic perception which are not so far recognized by the modern scientific world.

A careful analysis of the method of working followed by a scientist brings out the importance of mind, of intellect, as his most significant instrument. Mentally, that is intellectually, the scientist does his work, whereas a student of theosophy goes beyond his mind, he transcends the barrier of intellect and works with supra-mental faculties. But this generalization also is more apparent than real. As a matter of fact, even a scientist uses some faculties which transcend his mind. This does not imply that a scientist does not use his brain at all rather, it implies that when the function of intellectualization is over, a different layer of consciousness is activated and the necessary illumination takes place. The functioning of such supra-mental power has been experienced by many eminent scientists and they have stated so. Sir Jagadish Chandra Bose, the famous Indian botanist who demonstrated that even plants and metals have similar responses as that of the sentient beings, once stated, "This I know that no vision of truth can come except in the absence of all sources of distraction, and when the mind has reached the point of rest." Actually, when a scientist cognizes something universal underlying his observations, at that moment something else which is not within the ken of mind comes into activity. Thus even a scientist concerned with the discovery of relationships between physical phenomena makes use of supra-mental powers.

There are two types of knowledge that a man can acquire. They correspond in sanskrit to *Parā* and *Aparā Vidyā*. That which can be perceived by the five human senses is known as *Aparā Vidyā* and that which lies beyond and cannot be cognized by the five senses is known as *Parā Vidyā*. The latter, i.e. the *Parā Vidyā* lies beyond the frontiers of mind and can never be comprehended by it. Only that which is within the ken of mind and intellect can be grasped by the scientist or the philosopher using his brain. Whenever any beautiful idea, whether in the realm of science or of philosophy is grasped by an individual, it is a result of contact between the supramental faculties and the knowledge that lies beyond the five senses. It is necessary to rise beyond the activities of mind in order to grasp even a fragment of that knowledge. J. Krishnamurti has pointedly drawn our attention to the fact that Truth or Reality resides beyond the frontiers of mind. Generally, a scientist seems to ignore the function of the supra-mental faculty and artificially draws a line between Science and Theosophy or between Science and Philosophy.

A natural question arises as to how to go beyond the limits of mind. In order to go beyond mind, one has to be an occultist. One of the Masters of the Wisdom once wrote, "Life, after all, the greatest problem within the ken of human conception, is a mystery that the greatest of your men of science will never solve......It can never be grasped as long as it is studied separately and apart from Universal Life. To solve the great problem one has to become an occultist." As long as a scientist is concerned only with the form aspect of life and is satisfied with the discovery of the pattern of relationship between the various forms of life, he need not tread the path of occultism. But if he desires to study life itself and if he wants to study the causes behind the law of evolution, he has to become an occultist.

What is occultism ? Occultism means inner knowledge as distinguished from that which is known from outside. The knowledge which may be derived by the working of mind is only objective perception of a phenomenon. But there is a subjective reality too, which can be perceived only by coming into contact with the life within that phenomenon which is being studied. In order to explore both the objective and the subjective aspects of life, one must be a scientist as well as an occultist.

We are apt to think that life and form are distinct and separable characteristics of all objects in nature. But those who know tell us that in fact, life and form, the subjective and the objective Realities, always exist together. Therefore, neither of the two aspects can be compartmentalized, nor can they be studied properly in isolation. In order to have an integrated understanding of life and of various problems confronting mankind, it is necessary to have an idea of that subjective Reality, the Universal Life, which is pervading everything, and without which no knowledge can be considered as complete.

What is the nature of this Universal Life and how can we have a direct perception of That ? If universal Life is said to be beyond the reach of mind and if mind is the only instrument for acquiring knowledge that we have so far got, the process by which we can have direct perception of this Universal Life must be very difficult. It is indeed so. Two methods are suggested for it, but none of them is very easy. The first path is known as the Path of Occultism and the second the Path of Mysticism. Either of the paths would lead us to the understanding of the Universal Life or Truth. On the first path the unfoldment of the finer layers of consciousness is gradual. The aspirant passes through a series of "initiations" and step by step the various veils over his consciousness are rent. On this path, one has to seek his 'Master' and be his 'Disciple'. The path of the mystic is different. It is a flight from the alone to the Alone. The seeker on this path has just to leap into the realm of the unknown. There is no process, there is no learning and there is no "*Guru*" or "Master" for the aspirant on this path. On this path, the realization is spontaneous. But the courage to leap into the realm of the unknown is as difficult to acquire as the determination to follow the path of Occultism. Both the paths are difficult to follow. Only at the end of the stupendous journey there will be the understanding of the Universal Life, and only then the Truth will cast its veil aside. Till then, one will have to believe in and follow the teachings given by elders. Even the scientist has no escape from this method. If the scientist wants to know about the Universal Life, he also must follow the same course.

Understood in this way there is no artificial line, much less a contradiction, between science, philosophy and religion.

Now, a few words about religion. There seems much confusion and misunderstanding in modern scientific circles about religion and its relationship with philosophy. If philosophy is the theory of life and religion is the practice of it, if we can rightly understand the theory of life, then our entire living will change. Sometimes, even as we live in a particular way, our understanding about life changes and improves. A person, who out of fear or awe or wonder, worships trees, snakes, thunder, or the clouds, believes in his own simple way that the Universal Life pervades all these phenomena. A person may not have the direct perception of the grand vision of the mystic or the occultist, but it is possible that his belief may one day lead him to the position where he would have the unveiled perception of Reality. It is therefore useful and sometimes even necessary that we should suspend our judgement for the time being instead of vehemently attacking the so called blind beliefs of simple persons. All rituals, all mysteries and all beliefs have some value to certain individuals. Let scientists understand the problems of philosophy and religion, and let religious persons appreciate the problems of science. Let us have a balanced view on life, a right understanding, and a right conduct. In short, let us appreciate the value of everything in this world, and thus have atleast a glimpse or a fragmentary perception of the Universal Life.

III

"The evolution of matter is a rearrangement; the evolution of life is an unlocking and an unfoldment......From His fullness of Power, Love and Beauty, He gave to the first speck of life all that He is."

—C. Jinarajadasa.

ORIGIN OF LIFE

By

PROF. P. MAHESHWARI, D. SC., F. N. I.

Head of the Department of Botany

Delhi University, Delhi

Ancient and Medieval Beliefs

For many centuries people considerd that the earth was flat and immovable and that the sun circled round it, rising in the east and hiding itself behind the sea or the mountains in the west. Not only did the earth look flat but they also thought that it had to be so in order that God could see all the human beings at the same time. About living things, for example, insects, worms, and mice, they conjectured that these could not only be born from things like themselves but could also arise by spontaneous generation, out of mud, dung and earth. In ancient Egypt the view prevailed that the layer of silt left behind after the flooding of the Nile could give rise to living creatures when warmed by the sun. Frogs, toads, snakes, mice and even crocodiles were believed to originate in this way. In fact, at one time some perfectly sensible people thought that even the American Indians whose origin could not be traced clearly to Adam and Eve, must have come from the mud. People in villages and grandmothers in our homes still think that maggots arise from dung and rotting meat, and that various domestic pests arise of their own accord out of rubbish, mud and dirt.

In the 16th century van Helmont (1577-1644), the well-known mystic of Brussels who linked science with religion, used some experimental methods which enabled him to make substantial progress in the study of the problem of nutrition of plants. Nevertheless, he was convinced that living things could arise by spontaneous generation. He held that human sweat and wheat grains could serve as the life-giving principle. As a method of actually obtaining living organisms he suggested placing a dirty shirt in a receptacle containing wheat bran. He said that after 21 days the exhalations from the shirt together with those of the wheat would form living mice. He added with obvious pleasure that these artificially produced mice were of both sexes and exactly like those born from the "seed" of their parents.

Redi's Experiments

The experiments of the Tuscan physician Francesco Redi (1626-1697) formed the turning point. Redi had been reading in Homer's Iliad of the account of the death of Patroclus. Achilles was afraid of leaving his friend's body for fear that flies would come and foul the wounds. Redi decided to test the idea and in 1668 published the results of a simple experiment. He took cooked meat so that nothing remained alive in it and placed some pieces in each of three jars. One he left uncovered, the second was covered with parchment and the third with fine muslin. In the first jar maggots appeared in a few days but none in the second. Although plenty of flies alighted on the muslin covering the third jar, no maggots appeared in the meat. Redi observed how the flies laid their eggs on the muslin, but it is only when these eggs fell on to the meat that maggots developed inside it. From this he concluded that larvae do not generate spontaneously in the meat and that new flies arise from eggs laid by parent flies, the decaying substances being only a suitable place or a nest for the development of insects.

The Microbes :—About the same time as Redi carried out his famous experiments, a new world of living creatures invisible to the naked eye was opened up by the Dutch scientist, Anthony Van Leeuwenhoek (1632-1723). Originally a draper's assistant he later on took up the job of a janitor of the city Hall of Delft. His work there was rather light and he began to amuse himself with a new hobby of lens grinding. He made about 500 microscopes giving a magnification of nearly 270 times. With these microscopes, which were much superior to any of the previous ones, he began examining all kinds of things like a child in a strange room. In 1676, in a letter to the Royal Society of London he described in detail some 'living animalcules' found by him in rain water which had stood for a long time in the air, in various infusions, in excrement, and in the tartar of teeth. Continuing his observations, Leeuwenhoek gave descriptions of infusoria, yeasts, bacteria, sperms and red blood corpuscles.

The curious discoveries of Leeuwenhoek attracted considerable attention and provoked other studies of a similar nature. With this new tool of a microscope, biologists now found micro-organisms wherever decay or fermentation of organic substances was going on. They were found in all kinds of plant infusions and decoctions, such as decaying meat, stale broth, sour milk, fermenting liquors, and so on. As the belief in the spontaneous generation of living things was current at the time, it was the most natural thing to take it for granted that the microbes which were so much smaller than mice and insects could certainly arise from the inanimate matter in these decoctions and infusions.

The Welsh Roman Catholic priest and naturalist J. T. Needham (1713-1781) believed that in each microscopic particle of organic matter there was concealed a special 'vital force' which could animate the organic matter in an infusion. To prove his point he took a quantity of hot mutton gravy and shut it up in a phial closed tightly with a cork. This he heated further in hot ashes and yet after some days the vessel was teeming with microorganisms. Needham naturally concluded that it was not only possible, but inevitable that microorganisms should arise spontaneously from putrefying organic substances.

An Italian scientist and priest Spallanzani severely criticized Needham's conclusions. He asserted that Needham had not sufficiently heated the vessels containing the liquid, resulting in their inadequate sterilization. Spallanzani himself carried out hundreds of experiments in which plant decoctions and other organic liquids were subjected to prolonged boiling, after which the vessel containing them was sealed and thus the access of air to the liquids was prevented. Air, according to Spallanzani, carried the germs of microorganisms. Whenever the operation was conducted with proper attention the liquids contained in the vessel did not putrefy and living creatures did not appear in them.

The Work of Pasteur

The French Academy of Sciences announced a prize to anyone who could throw light on the primary origin of living creatures. This prize was awarded to Louis Pasteur who, in 1862, after a series of conclusive experiments, demonstrated the impossibility of the spontaneous formation of microorganisms from the various infusion and solutions of organic substances. He was succesful in doing this only because he left the beaten track of blind empiricism and approached the whole problem more broadly and critically.

To satisfy the objections of Needham, Pouchet and some others Pasteur half filled a flask with the experimental liquid, then softened the neck of the flask in a flame and drew it out laterally in the shape of the letter S. The contents of the flask were then boiled. When a strong current of steam issued from the mouth of the side tube, the boiling was stopped and the flask was allowed to cool. With this treatment the contents of the flask remained unchanged although the solution was directly connected through the curved neck with the surrounding atmosphere. This was because all particles of dust, including microorganisms, were retained in the curved part of the S-shaped tube.

When the neck was cut off, microorganisms soon appeared in the liquid.

Further, Pasteur showed that the content of microorganisms in the air was by no means constant but changed according to the season and place. The largest number of germs is present in the air of towns and inhabited places. The air of fields and forests is less rich in microorganisms and finally on the mountains, especially at great heights, the number of these minute living creatures floating in the air is quite insignificant. One may, therefore, open flasks containing sterile liquids without their being exposed to much infection. In many cases such flasks remained sterile after resealing, although untreated mountain air had been admitted to them.

Pasteur also demonstrated that the air is far from being the only source of infection of organic liquids. Germs are present on the surfaces of all the objects which are used in the course of an experiment. Therefore, these must be meticulously disinfected.

All subsequent attempts to find examples of spontaneous generation of living organisms, however small, were in vain. This is quite understandable for microorganisms are not just lumps of organic material but have a very delicate and complicated organization. It is impossible to believe that complicated structures of this sort could emerge in the course of a short time before our eyes out of structureless solutions of organic substances. The hypothesis is, in essence, just as absurd as that frogs arise from dew or lions from the stones of the desert.

Having discarded the theory of spontaneous generation, biologists were, however, left without any alternative explanation. The only other way life could come is by special creation but science denies the supernatural. In 1821 some people made a bold attempt to "solve" the tangle by saying that the original forms of life came from some other planet. This idea was taken up quite enthusiastically by Liebig, Richter, Kelvin and Arrhenius. However, such a view does not explain anything but merely banishes the investigation of the question to some conveniently inaccessible corner of the universe.

All the same, the possibility of life on other worlds may still be examined. Neptune, Uranus, Saturn and Jupiter have cloud-like surfaces and low temperatures (-100°C); Mercury lacks water and atmoshphere and undergoes wide temperature fluctuations; and Venus lacks water and oxygen. Only on Mars, which has O_2, CO_2, H_2O, and temperatures from 10-15°C to freezing, there have been seen some seasonal variations in colour from green in spring to brown in autumn. From this it has been concluded that plants are present in Mars, and if plants, possibly also animals. However, it is doubtful if the extreme cold and dryness and the lethal radiations of interstellar space would permit life to be transferred on meteorites from one planet to another. Possibly spores and microorganisms could, but then the questions arises how were they generated on Mars itself.

The Viruses :—A new lead to the concept of origin of life was given in the 20th century by the discovery and purification of viruses. These are much smaller (10-300 microns) than the bacteria and are also of a much simpler chemical composition. At least some of them seem to consist of but one substance, nucleoprotein, although even this is extremely complex in its organization. Several viruses, have been purified, including that of poliomyelitis, and crystallized, and they have the power of mutation and self-duplication. They are thus on the borderland between the living and the non-living.

However, the viruses as we know them at present can exist only within a living cell and at the expense of the material produced by that cell. If the first living things were more or less like viruses, they must have been different from those we know today for they must have fed upon non-living matter. Such viruses would form the probable link between the molecular world and the world of cells, i.e. between the inorganic and the organic, between the inanimate and the animate.

When Did Life Begin ?

The next question is when were these original nucleo-proteins formed ? It seems reasonable to think that this happened after the earth's crust had cooled. Perhaps it can be narrowed still further to the time when liquid water could lie on the crust. The oldest recognized surface rocks (Archaeozoic) are estimated to be 1500 million years old. One method of such calculations depends on the assumption that certain minerals initially contained no lead but gained it from the radio-active decay of uranium. By knowing the rate of decay and the present concentrations of uranium and lead it is possible to make some estimate of their age.

The next point is when did the first fossil forms of life appear? The fossil record goes back to the Cambrian, about 500 million years ago but there are various structures in the Pre-cambrian and even in the Archean rocks that some authorities interpret as traces left by simple organisms such as calcareous algae. However, even these simplest organisms, if we compare them with similar forms of life today, must have had as complete a range of biochemical organization as those that are more complex. Now, so far the study of evolution has been the study of evolution of form and structure because that is what leaves a fossil record. There must have been a phase in the earth's history in which biochemical evolution was an active process. The time occupied by this phase is anybody's guess but it was probably as long as the morphological phase and it may be concluded that life of some sort has probably existed for 1,000 million years or more.

Now, granting that this was so, did life originate once only and did all other species evolve from the original one or have there been constant new origins? The basic similarities in the physiology of present day organisms in spite of the structural dissimilarities lead one to think that life originated but once and then as the result of gradual evolution it led to the present different forms of life.

A natural query is that if life originated in those ancient times, can it not originate now? Some Russian investigators, Boshian and Olga Lepeshinskaya, claim to have seen bacteria and cells appear from non-living matter such as the yolk of egg and organic substances in decomposition, but critical investigators consider those reports untrustworthy. One difficulty is that even if spontaneous generation were to take place at the moment, we would hardly be able to recognize it. We do not know in what type of medium this is likely to happen nor the manner in which it will manifest itself. Another objection is that two billion years ago there was probably no free oxygen thus making it possible for organic compounds to remain stable for long periods and enable the change from non-living to living. Today organic compounds would disintegrate after a while due to the presence of oxygen.

How Did It Happen?

What we regard as impossible on the basis of ordinary human experience is meaningless in the present context. Given two billion years the impossible can become possible, and the possible becomes probable.

One can only speculate as to what may have been the probable steps in the evolution of life. The sequence must have been: (a) synthesis of organic compounds; (b) synthesis of more complex organic molecules; (c) production of proteins and enzymes; (d) the organization of a cell with metabolic properties; and (e) evolution of more advanced organisms. While this looks highly theoretical, a few steps here and there in the synthesis of organic molecules have been successfully carried out in the laboratory. For example, Miller (1953) in the U.S.A. showed that by passing a high-voltage electric spark through a mixture of hydrogen, methane, ammonia and water it was possible to obtain urea and several amino acids. Another American biochemist, Sydney Fox, heated some anhydrous mixtures of amino acids and obtained large peptide molecules whose molecular weights range up to 20,000. Further, in certain solutions these peptides aggregated into little spherules which are quite suggestive of cells although lacking the structural and biochemical complexity of normal cells. While this is highly significant, no one has yet synthesized any enzymes. These are the catalysts of life which have no doubt been obtained in pure form from living organisms but which have not yet been produced in vitro. Further, these are irreversibly inactivated by heat and could not arise by heating amino acids.

Present day theories of the biosynthesis of proteins postulate that nucleic acids are the fundamental templates upon which amino acids are arranged and united into protein molecules. However, so far very little experimental evidence is available about the hypothetical chemical evolution of nucleic acids or even their components, the purines and pyrimidines.

Granted that there were proteins and enzymes of various kinds, the next step is the evolution of the cell. How was the cell-membrane formed and how did the nuceoproteins become incorporated in it? To this we have no real answer. Some cell-like structures have no doubt been made artificially but these lack the property of metabolizing and reproducing themselves. A real *jeevanu* must have a battery of enzymes, an osmotic membrane, and the capacity to duplicate itself. When some clever scientist has done this, synthetic life may be said to have started. Those with chlorophyll in addition to the other components could be said to give rise to plants, and those without chlorophyll to animals. No one has yet succeeded in doing this artificially but with the earnestness with which this problem is now being studied, we should be able to know the essential steps in the process in about a hundred years from now.

LIFE IN PLANTS

By

SHRI A. C. MUKHERJEE

Department of Chemical Engineering & Technology
Delhi Polytechnic, Delhi

There are two theories of the origin of life on our planet that are not based on direct supernatural intervention. One of these is that life in simple form came to the earth from another planet or planetary system. Few scientists accept this theory, because even if a living particle could travel through space, there is some doubt that it could survive the extreme cold and the exposure to lethal ultra-violet light. The alternative theory is that life arose on the earth from the non-living matter. This could have happened two to three billion years ago, when the cooling planet had reached a stage—warmer than at present, but not too warm for simple matter—at which fairly complex chemical compounds could have formed spontaneously. The steps between the non-living and the living matter were probably gradual, but must have involved sooner or later the formation of enzymes and of substance that could reproduce themselves.

Evidence for the theory that life arose on the earth from the non-living matter comes in part from the fact that every chemical element that occurs in living matter is also a common constituent of the non-living matter. Other evidence comes from the fact that fairly complex compounds do form spontaneously under certain external conditions that may have been present as our planet cooled. We must remember, however, that theories of the origin of life are in the realm of pure speculation.

Let us see life in its simplest forms. All living things are characterized by the presence of a complex substance called 'Protoplasm.' Protoplasm is that which is 'alive' in animals and plants. We do not yet know as to what is it that makes Protoplasm alive. It can be said that aliveness or life is a transcendental force not inherent in the chemical composition of protoplasm or that life is due to the single compound characteristic of protoplasm and is a result of peculiar aggregations of compounds occurring in the protoplasm.

Protoplasm was first recognized as a living substance by the French zoologist Dujardin in 1835; it was, however, given the name Protoplasm by the Bohemian zoologist Purkinje in 1839. This terms was brought into general use among scientists by the German botanist Von Mohl. Protoplasm was called the 'physical basis of life' by T. H. Huxley.

Protoplasm has got a complex composition of inorganic and organic compounds dissolved in water and there are suspended droplets of insoluble liquids and particles of insoluble solids. These can be classified as (1) Inorganic salts such as chlorides, nitrates, phosphates, and sulphates, (2) Organic compounds such as (a) carbohydrates (sugar), (b) Lipins (Lipoids) including True Fats such as Glyceryl Esters of Fattyacids—Olein (Waxes), Phosphorized Fats, and Sterols or Solid Alcohols, (3) Proteins, (4) Metabolites and (5) Nucleic Acids. In this way, protoplasm exhibits some unique physical and chemical properties which can be termed as 'Biological Characterics', because they have no counterpart in the non-living world.

Acharya Jagadish Chandra Bose emerged as one of the earliest bio-physicists who applied physical means to study physiological problems. He confined himself to the field of plant physiology. In his opinion plants were intermediate beings between the living and the non-living and he considered them "highly complicated but fundamentally simple". By his rare genius he constructed wonder ful instruments and traced every sign of life in plants, found out the mode of their responses to stimulations traced their nervous system and obtained the evidence of irritability, recorded their rates of growth and proved beyond doubt the existence of many other wonderful symptoms which is identified with life. His apparatus 'Crescograph' and 'Resonant Recorder' were liked by every scientist of the world and every one was struck by the delicacy of these instruments. In fact, Prof. Molisch of Vienna wrote, "I saw the plant writing down the rate of assimilation of its gaseous food. I also observed the speed of the impulse of excitation in the plant being recorded by the Resonant Recorder, which automatically records intervals of time as short as a thousandth part of a second. All these are more wonderful than fairy tales;

nevertheless, those who have the opportunity of seeing the experiments become fully convinced that they are laboratory miracles revealing the hitherto invisible reactions underlying life". By such a wonderful discovery Sir Jagadish Chandra Bose impressed the world, and by his further researches he continued to impress the scientists of the age.

Sir Jagadish Chandra Bose at first showed that there is no difference in responses of the living and the non-living. Then he showed that there is no difference between the nervous life of plants and animals. He also showed that the plant called *mimosa pudica*, which is commonly known as *Lajjabati*, is just like a human being. In fact all plants are like human beings: if we give them blow, they feel it; if we make them drink poison, it has the same effect, both on them and on human beings. The plants sleep in the night and wake up in the morning. They even suffer death like men.

Mimosa Pudica was extensively used by Sir Jagadish Chandra Bose for studying the responses of plants to external stimulation. When a branch of this plant is touched, the leaves are closed and the branch droops. This is explained by the fact that any disturbance to the plant spreads out all over the body of the plant in the form of invisible electrical waves. Consequently, there is contraction of tissues lying on one side of the branch. Thus the branch droops. It is just like an outward bending of one of the metals having more linear expansion than the other when both are coupled together and is subjected to heat. In case of other trees like mango, coconut and *jamun* etc. a different type of disturbance is created. The tissues which are present all around the branch are contracted. Thus the effect is uniform and the branch does not fall. But if the tissues present on the upper side of it are made unconscious by chloroform, the same branch on touching now falls. A plant is said to be dead when it fails to respond to external stimuli, that is, when no curves are recorded by the instrument.

The ascent of sap-solution to a height of 400 ft. against the pull of gravity, as in the case of an eucalyptus tree is also wonderful. It is carried out by the working of living cells present in vascular channel, which create a continuous pulsation. The pulsation can be detected by to and fro movement of the needle of the galvanometer, when it is put in a circuit with the plant. This pulsation is compared with the beating of the heart in animals.

The ancient thinkers knew well that life and mind exist everywhere in essence and vary only by the degree and the manner of their emergence and functioning. All is in all. It is out of the complete involution that the complete evolution progressively appears. The privilege of initiating one of the most important discoveries by which the experimental science is confirming the wisdom of our forefathers went to Dr. J. C. Bose who interested himself in this type of research when it was practically unknown in India and very much less developed in other parts of the world. Like all pioneers, Dr. Bose faced handicaps of money, tradition and public apathy, but undaunted he proceeded and overcame the difficulties. After years of hard work he could show to the world during the first quarter of the twentieth century that there is not much difference between an animal and a tree, between the living and the so-called non-living forms of life. That was a scientific demonstration of the Vedantic view of life stressing unity in all forms of existence. Indeed, One Life is the source of all life.

THE INVISIBLE MAN

By

DR. M. H. DESAI, PH. D. (LONDON)
Department of Applied Science
Delhi Polytechnic, Delhi

When the physical man dies, something goes out of him. Various names such as soul, spirit, life, etc. are given to that which goes out of the human body. That which goes out is not lost, rather, that gives the idea of the existence of early lives of the individual.

There is a science of spiritualism. Spiritualism here does not mean only religious. What is active energy or power in man is called spirit in Christianity and hence the science of the spirit of man is called the science of spiritualism. That which deals with that spirit of man is called spiritualism and the phenomenon dealing with that spirit is called spiritualistic phenomenon. The room in which such experiments are carried out and where the spiritualistic phenomenon occurs is called the *seance*.

There are certain conditions for that room on which the success of the spiritualistic phenomenon depends. These conditions depend upon the rules of the Astral World. The room should be dimly lighted or should be completely dark. Bright light is not allowed in these experiments. Certain persons who do not believe in spiritualism do not like this condition but this is according to the scientific principles of the Astral World. There is nothing like a fraud or cheating in these phenomena. The Theosophical Society has explained the principles according to which partial materialization of the Astral matter takes place; the vibrations of strong light are unhelpful for this. In presence of bright light, materialization cannot take place, hence the light should be dim. Bright day light is also objectionable, hence these experiments are carried out either in the evenings or at night in presence of dim-light.

Bishop C. W. Leadbeater, who was an authority on the science of spiritualism and who has interpreted all the various phenomena in the light of the principles of Theosophy, says that these experiments are very simple. What you require is a round table, one central-legged if possible otherwise a three-legged round table may do. Time of the experiment should be evening or night, but should never be in the bright day light or in the presence of bright lights. There should be atleast three persons. The results of these experiments will be successful if these conditions are followed. At least three persons should place their hands on the round table with their palms touching the top of the table. Some people use a wooden board or *planchette*, as it is called. There should be a paper on which the letters of the alphabet are given on the circumference and there should be figures from 0 to 9 on this round chart. Some people use a hat upside down with the brim upwards. The minds of the members watching these phenomena should be calm and they should have no anxiety or too much of curiosity for the results of these experiments. Some patience is also required as the experiments do not start at once but take a few minutes. After a patient and silent watching for a few minutes, it is found that the hat or the planchette moves of its own accord and gives reply to your questions by tapping or by movements of the hat towards the letters on the chart. Some code words are made to interpret the tapping sound, as for example, one tap means 'yes' and two taps mean 'no'. There should be no idea of challenging in your mind. Sometimes, it happens that when you raise your hand, the hat is lifted from the table and somtimes the whole table with the hat is lifted a few inches from the ground.

Eminent scientists like Sir Oliver Lodge and Sir William Crooks, have observed the phenomena and they have convinced themselves that there is no fraud or trick in these. A certain amount of force is coming from the dead people and they give reply to our questions. Sometimes the answers are correct, sometimes the answers are wrong. If there is a weak-minded person in the group, the dead man's spirit takes possesson of the body of the weak-minded person and through him gives answer to the questions. The weak-minded person is called in such cases a 'medium' and his voice or face sometimes changes. Sometimes, the medium falls in a sort of sleep and in that unconscious or trance condition he gives reply to the questions put to him. The spirit of the dead people have no physical body hence, they want to express themselves by taking possession of the physical body of the medium. Such mediums can do a drawing or can do even a painting and he can also give an information which may be concerning far off places and events that took place a few years before.

Sir Oliver Lodge, who had lost his young son in the World War I, could get some information about him which was not known to other members of the group. Sir William Crookes, who also did not believe in the life after death was convinced that there is a soul which continues after the death of the physical body and it can give some information through spiritualistic phenomena. These eminent scientists were not able to understand these spiritualistic phenomena but when they came in contact with Madam H. P. Blavatsky, Col. H.S. Olcott and Bishop C.W. Leadbeater who explained to them the principles of Theosophy and the science of the Astral World, they became convinced that there was life after death and that every human being has an invisible astral body. In the astral world, the dead man with his astral body can work with a tremendous velocity and can travel very fast. He can read the thoughts of the dead or of the living persons and can pass even through solid walls. Just as water can pass through a sieve, so can astral matter pass through a wall. Physical objects are no hindrance to the astral matter.

For such phenomena in which materialization takes place, great concentration of mind is needed and ordinary people are not able to do so. Those who have achieved great *Siddhis* can do this. Astral matter travels at a very great speed. There were experiments done where Indian flowers were brought to England and were made to grow in a sand box and were photographed.

For this type of partial or complete materialization astral matter is needed and this matter is taken mainly from the body of the medium and to a small extent from the bodies of the other members who are present there. Due to this, the medium feels too much exhausted after the sitting of the *seance*, he feels like the a patient who has undergone a major operation. Therefore, these experiments should not be tried for a long time. These experiments are injurious so they should not be done in a professional way. All the members who attend the *seance* are more or less affected.

Partial materialization is such that it cannot be photographed. You may hear the voice but you will not be able to know whence it is coming. But when there is complete materialization, it can be photographed with due permission of the man incharge of the phenomenon. Such complete materialization is more difficult and rquires strong will power and concentration. When such experiments of either partial materialization or complete materialization are in progress, no body should disturb either by shouting or touching the medium or by putting on a switch of light or by a torch etc. This suddenly gives a shock to the medium and may be dangerous to him. During the process of materialization, astral matter is going out of the body of the medium and when the materialized body disappears, the astral matter is returned to the body of the medium. When this process is going on, no body should disturb by putting on a light as the strong vibrations of a bright light hinder the movement of the astral matter.

Similarly, no member of the group should ask the materialized body to move far away from the medium. The materialized body is always as a rule very near the medium and no body should try to take it far away.

Now, let us see what should be the attitude of those who attend the meetings of sprititualism. It should not be of too much curiosity, challenging or distrust. It should be a desire to find out the truth. They should know that the physical body of a man is like an overcoat. The dead man has an astral sight and with that sight he can tell what has happened in the past, at a great distance or many years earlier.

Thought reading is also possible and some phenomena belong to thought reading. Some things which are lost, or misplaced are found out by this process. The mediums are even able to read out a letter which is in a locked box.

There are certain explanations given of these phenomena. One of the explanations is that the astral matter can pass through physical matter. In this physical world there are only three dimensions : length, breadth and height or depth. But in the astral world there are four dimensions. It is very difficult to describe the nature of the fourth dimension. It can only be experienced by those who have the astral sight. Fourth dimension has also been explained by eminent mathematicians.

Spiritualistic societies do not necessarily know the explanations of these phenomena, specially as given by Theosophy. There is a vast amount of literature on spiritualism and those who are interested in this subject are advised to refer to some of the books written by unprejudiced persons.

(Reference : Spiritualism and Theosophy by C. W. Leadbeater. Published by Theosophical Publishing House, Adyar, Madras, India.)

CONCERNING MAN AND HIS FUTURE

By

SHRI BEPIN BEHARI

Premashram, Motihari, Bihar

Even today there are many things concerning man which are not very well explained. Researches in the physical science and studies in human psychology have unveiled many mysteries about the universe and the man, still much more remains to be known. Modern scientists have not yet been able to explore adequately many fields of human experiences such as fortune-telling, dream interpretation, psychic perception and many other occult relationships. Many eminent persons such as Mrs. Annie Besant, Rev. C. W. Leadbeater, Bro. C. Jinarajadasa, Mr. Geoffrey Hodson and Mrs. Phoebe D. Bendit and others have done much work in this regard. Nonetheless, much more still remains to be done. In this talk a very small fragment of the subject will be dealt with.

Human body is made of various chemicals: for example, it consists of oxygen 72%, carbon 13.4%, hydrogen 9.1%, nitrogen 2.5%, calcium 1.3%, phosphorus 1.25% and many other chemicals in small quantities. But merely a combination of these chemicals does not produce a man. A man is something more than these chemicals;

what is that something more is not yet well known. Many names are given to that: some call it Life and others call it Spirit. Whatever name is given to it, it actually denotes the force which gives sensitivity to every nerve cell in the human body. It is this force which gives the capacity of growth; it is the absence of this force that makes the man dead and inert. This is the energy which sustains every form of manifestation. It is difficult to describe the essential nature of this energy, but its existence cannot be denied. The scientists present at the international symposium held at Moscow in 1956 to discuss the problem of *The Origin of Life on the Earth* "realized that they could neither define, nor unequivocally recognize 'life' but they were nevertheless certain that there was such an entity to be recognized". According to *The Secret Doctrine,* Spirit is coeternal with Matter. "Once we pass from Absolute Negation", it is stated, "duality supervenes in the contrast of Spirit (or Consciousness) and Matter, Subject and Object. Spirit and Matter are, however, to be regarded, not as independent realities, but as the two symbols or aspects of the Absolute." We may regard Matter and Spirit as the two aspects of a unity which is not subject to death or decay.

An understanding of the problems relating to the invisible part of the human personality, the survival after death, and the relationship between Superconsciousness and the evolution of man gives us an insight into the nature and function of man. It may also enable us to recognize the vast realm of spiritual development that is destined for each humanbeing.

It is common to experience exaltation or depression in some person's company. There are persons whose nearness pleases us, and there are others who repel. Many persons are inspiring and sympathetic, others are gloomy and inimical. It has also been observed that many places have powerful influences: by going to a religious place or by attending some rituals, very often one gets a strange feeling of upliftment. Uncommon satisfaction has been very often felt at places which had been the *ashramas* of evolved saints. These experiences are ordinarily explained as psychological responses. These explanations are, however, not adequate. They elude the real or the causal relationships. They do not enable an individual to produce such influences at will. Satisfactory explanation of these phenomena can be found on the basis of the knowledge of the hidden sides of things. There are many unknown dimensions of every event. There are invisible magnetic radiations from every individual and from every place. Perception of these radiations depends on the degree of sensitivity of the individual. The attractive or the repulsive nature of a person is due to the nature of the invisible bodies of the person, which are classified into seven sub-divisions, namely, physical, astral or emotional, mental, intuitional, spiritual, monadic, and divine bodies of the individual. (Cf. Man and His Bodies by Mrs. Annie Besant). These seven bodies can again be grouped together under three categories, namely, physical, psychological and the psychic bodies of the man.

That which can be seen with our eyes and felt with our five senses may be considered as physical in nature. There are many physical things which are perceived only with the aid of scientific instruments, but in such cases, the scientific instruments assist in increasing the capacity of human sense-perception. Very often our unaided senses do not register the complete picture, and scientific instruments are required to overcome this shortcoming. The experiments carried by Dr. Walter B. Kilner of St. Mary's Hospital, London concerning the human atmosphere have been done in the same way. With our physical eyes it was not possible to observe the extra-physical counterpart of an individual, but Dr. Kilner tried to photograph it with the aid of coloured screens. He has recorded his findings in a book *The Human Aura*. This research indicated that each individual has got an atmoshphere, which is more or less invisible. This invisible atmosphere of the man can, however, be perceived. The nature and composition of the human aura thus discovered depended upon the personal life of the individual. The invisible portion of the human body as discovered by Dr. Kilner resembles that portion of the individual which was called as the etheric body by the Theosophical clairvoyants. (Col. A.W. Powell's *The Etheric Double* is a very illuminating book on the subject.)

The psychological portion of the humanbeing consists mainly of his thoughts and emotions. There is a mechanism by which emotions and thoughts of one individual are transmitted to another person. This is possible because emotions and thoughts of an individual, in fact, are physical in their nature, but the substance of which they are made of is of very very fine density. The emotion and thought 'stuffs' resemble clouds of different colours depending on the precision and content of the thought and feeling. These stuffs have their own rules of action and reaction. The (psychological) atmosphere of any place depends very much on the nature of these emotion and thought stuffs. The serenity of the place of worship, or the confusion at a railway station is explained by the presence of devotional or confused astro-mental stuffs at these places. The confusion created by the innumerable passengers produces such chaotic vibrations that the very atmosphere is coloured by them. Even hours after these passengers are gone, the atmosphere is so much surcharged that subsequent visitors are influenced by it depending, of course, on the amount of corresponding emotional and thought stuffs present in their own personality.

A recent scientific instrument called Electro-Encephelograph has greatly helped in bringing out the psychological make-up of an individual. This is a very simple instrument run by electricity. On the basis of experiments carried out with the help of this instrument, it appears that the reaction of the brain of every individual is as unique as his finger-prints. The graph as recorded by the individual indicates his emotional characteristics of self-indulgence or restrain, confidence and such other character traits. No amount of coaching can change these individual responses. Even under hypnosis when the individual has his eyes closed but is reacting as if his eyes are open, the instrument will record the actual state, not as induced by hypnosis. The findings of this instrument has opened many so far closed avenues of human personality and one of the important conclusions is that brain of an individual is very much different from his mind. So the problem arises as to what is mind and what is brain. An important contribution of this experiment is the hypothesis that the physical and the psychological counterparts of the individual though interconnected are two distinct parts of the human personality.

Today, there is much ignorance regarding the psychic world and the psychic body. It is difficult to explain psychism and the psychic phenomena. Faculties commonly known as clairvoyance, psychometry, and the like are due to the psychic nature of the man. Psyche is that principle in man which enables him to understand intuitively the essential nature of things. There are many undifferentiated sense-organs in a human-being which make it possible for him to acquire psychic power. In some individuals the psychic sense is very much developed and they function on this level of consciousness with perfect awareness. (Phoebe D. Payne and Dr. Laurence J. Bendit have very well described the mechanism of psychic consciousness in their book entitled *The Psychic Sense.*)

The laws governing the physical health of an individual are well known. Towards the end of the last century attempts were made to discover the rules governing the psychological health of a man as well. Psychoanalysis and psychotherapy under mentally and emotionally balanced doctors have been effective in correcting imbalance in one's personality. But this branch of study itself is still in its infancy; the knowledge about the psychic health of a person is still very little known. Further researches in the domain of psychic well-being and consequently the discovery of the laws governing the psychic world and the psychic health of the individual will greatly modify the modern approach to human personality.

The physical, psychological and the psychic bodies of the man determine the nature and extent of experinece he is capable of. The inner man needs personality for its expression and that is provided by these vehicles. But there are other factors too, which influence the life of an individual. Physical characteristics are inherited from parents, racial characteristics and family traits (physical) link the individual with his ancestors. The society and the associations to which the individual belongs to influence his psychological make-up. Many national and parochial prejudices are the result of group thinking. Each society with which the individual is related to has a powerful influence on him, but there are other influences too which are not very well appreciated in the modern age.

Ordinarily, any belief in the influence of stars and planets is considered as superstition. The distant tiny stars flickering dimly are very often denied to have such a great influence on the individual as to control his limbs, emotions and thoughts. But this is a misconception; in fact, the influence of stars and planets is substantial. For example, the relationship between tides and the phases of the moon is well known. The lunar influence on the emotional life of an individual is being gradually recognized. Rudolf Thiel while describing the relationship between the starry heaven and the terrestrial life has recorded that "the menstrual period in women may be in some way under the domination of the heavenly body that divides time into months for us. For in the animal world also there occur periodic rhythms, all of a sexual nature, which seem linked with the Moon". In support of his contention he quotes the examples of sea urchins of the Riviera coast, eels in Florida and Japan, and the palolo worms in Samoan and Fiji islands. He has further stated that "the relationship between the cosmic order and the life rhythm of terrestrial beings brings to our notice a great deal of attention which was suddenly focussed upon Schwabe's sunspot periods when the correlation between them and the cycles of magnetic storms and northern lights was recognized." "Here was a new tie", Rudolf Thiel wrote, "mysteriously linking us to the Sun, which nourishes all life on Earth". Truly, the man has many unknown depths to his life and he is connected with many unknown force centres. Mr. N. Sri Ram has stated, "Even Science seems to think that man is a sphinx posing questions which we have not been able to answer so far. Man is a mystery, a miracle (according to Carlyle), difficult to probe and read, and greatly varying because of the compositeness of his nature."

Let us now consider what happens when an individual dies. "The mere physical expiry, apart from any precedent conditions due to disease, is not, according to such evidence as there is, a particularly difficult experience. In life there is deployment of the consciousness (along with his nature and tendencies) which for the time is the man. At death, and beginning even before it, there is a process of withdrawal, the faculties function less and less, untill there comes the point of extinction at which we say the man is dead". When life is withdrawn from the physical, it resides in the astral and mental bodies of the individual. Consciousness continues on these planes for a considerable period of time the duration of which depends upon the amount of energy put into them during the course of his physical existence. Later on, life is withdrawn from them as well and the consciousness falls into a state comparable to that of deep sleep; emotion and thought stuffs are cast aside but the carcasses of thoughts and emotions continue for sometime as a result of inertia. These carcasses sometimes appear as spooks and apparitions. After a period of rest in this state of blissful forgetfulness, the consciousness of the individual—the Ego—comes back again and takes various psychological and physical vestures the nature of which is determined by the experience the Ego has gathered during its earlier incarnations, the *karmic* limitations imposed on it, and the lesson it has to learn in the ensuing incarnation so that the Ego comes a little closer to its archetype. These are finely adjusted by the Lords of Karma. Thus the individual "comes back as a sweet innocent child, to begin a new chapter, to write in new characters a better story with more sense and more beautiful sentences". Life swings between birth and death not once but many times.

The subject of death and its meaning is one of deep importance to all of us. Men fear death, and it has been called the King of Terrors. In many books there are detailed descriptions of the after-death states, but they are all in some manner akin to dreaming. "Our life is but a sleep and a forgetting". Mr. N. Sri Ram, has stated, "If we can realize that death is a matter of time and there is unity only beyond the processes of time, we may look upon death with kindly eyes, as upon a friend". He has also indicated that it is by death of the existing forms that Nature is able to move forward to other and better forms. It is by continuing the old tendencies that the child-like simplicity is lost and the man shows characteristics which one could not have suspected to be there in the child. "It only means", Mr. N. Sri Ram has further stated that, "we have not died enough". The liberated man does not carry anything over; he has settled his account and in his inner nature is fresh and pure all the time. After successive births and deaths each individual has to attain this state of liberation.

During the course of evolution the man develops his latent powers and ultimately becomes a superman. This process of unfoldment relates more to the expansion of consciousness than to his physical bodies. There are many higher beings in this world who have transcended human limitations and have attained super-human powers. These higher-beings are maintaining contact with the terrestrial world and are helping the evolution of its inhabitants. It is possible to have direct contact with these Adepts. This is possible by refining the various vehicles of our experience. If the seven force-centres in a human body, which are known as the *chakras* in yogic literature, are energized and made active, it would be possible to have direct experiences of the occult nature. The process of energizing these force-centres has been referred to in ancient scriptures as the arousing of the 'serpent fire' or the *kundalini shakti*. This power is latent in every individual, but its development requires much sacrifice. The price has to be paid for every *siddhi* acquired. An aspirant is tested and tempted at every step on the occult path; every individual is to pass the vale of shadow before reaching the glorious land of omniscience and omnipotence. Many people fail on the way. That is why the path of occultism is strewn with the wrecks of neophytes. However, people have succeeded and what a man has done, a man can do, so there is every chance for each individual to ultimately succeed. When the final goal is attained it would be possible for the aspirant to know directly the way the cosmic consciousness, the angelic hosts and the perfected beings are constantly helping the individual to fulfil his destiny.

The indirect method of enquiry into the relationship between the divine consciousness and the evolution of the terrestrial world necessitates a very careful and objective study of the human society. The theory of evolution is already accepted and the scientists are trying to discover the pattern of growth. The great Russian occultist, Madam H.P. Blavatsky who founded the Theosophical

Society in 1875, stated in *The Secret Doctrine* that the plan of evolution proceeded in seven-fold nature : "The spiritual or divine, the psychic or semi-divine, the intellectual, the passional, the instinctual or cognitional, the semi-corporeal and the purely material or physical natures." Ethonological studies concerning the different races like the Polarians, Hyperboreans, Lemurians, Atlanteans and the Aryans have suggested that the origin and growth of races reveal the same pattern as suggested in *The Secret Doctrine*. The rise and fall of civilizations as well as the great seisemic changes are also connected with this pattern of evolution. Religion and philosophy, administration and education, society and culture all are closely related to this general scheme of growth. Here it may be indicated that there is some conscious energy behind this pattern of evolution, and that energy is sweetly and gently guiding the course of human destiny. We can experience this relationship and help the evolutionary forces, or we can deny its very existence and go on living our egocentric life. This, however, would not change the fact that the human individuals form only a tiny fragment of the great plan. Our free-will as understood in the popular sense of the term, is a myth, and the working of the God's Plan, which is evolution, is a fact. We experience pain, when we work against this plan. Even in order to escape human miseries, it is useful to discover the Great Law and to conform to it.

It is being increasingly realized that there is a definite goal to which the world is progressing.

An eminent French biologist, Jean Rostand in the book *Can Man be Modified*? has mentioned that the man is already moving towards attaining the quality of superman, and it is suggested in this book that we can assist this if we try to "make him more intelligent, sensitive, more disposed to solidarity and altruism, in a word more human". The Harvard Research on Creative Altruism has collected biographies of more than 4,000 saints of all ages and all lands and on that basis it was found out that these saints were better than their contemporaries even with regard to their physical well-being. Furthermore, "the law that love begets love was tested experimentally among the sworn enemies at an American college and a psychopathic hospital, and the positive power of love was found to destroy the hate between enemies". While explaining the mechanism of this relationship, Dr. C. Trew stated that "the essential unity of all that exists in the universe gives the power to altruism. This power is illimitable but an individual who is motivated from personal psyche, who is self centred and is concerned only with his petty interest cannot establish a rapport with this Universal Spirit". The present trend is towards developing this quality of altruism in human beings. This also is in conformity with the predetermined pattern of human evolution. The destiny of man is to attain the archetypal form that is predetermined for him. For this, he has to unfold his consciousness, discover his latent powers, and to establish right relationship with super-human beings—the Masters of the Wisdom, the Adept Brotherhood—

who want themselves to be known as "Elder Brethren".

Today, mankind is at a cross-road. One is required to choose between the material and the spiritual values. The choice is difficult to make. On the one side, the temptation is great, on the other the futility of possession is experienced. In order to grasp the full significance of spiritual life one has to cultivate a very high level of sensitivity and refinness. The path is not easy, but no one has claimed it to be so. Nonetheless, it is the only way for the salvation of the mankind. The easiest method to strengthen one-self in order to face the ordeal of the path is to cultivate deliberately the quality of impersonal love. This is a state of feeling in which the "inner man" comes out : it brings the inner without. Possibly, in the earlier stages of development, the impersonal love may have to be learnt by involving oneself and suffering for the personal possessive attachments. At a later stage, the personal attachments may be sublimated to the love for birds and trees, the appreciation of beautiful sunset or a landscape, in which the beholder forgets himself in rapture. This sublimation may help the individual to get a flash of the universal consciousness, which is an experience of unity amidst diversity. But it must be noted that love cannot be forced on anyone, nor can it be artificially cultivated: it is a virtue of the heart, a state of fulfilment of one's being. The feeling has to be spontaneous. Realization of the purpose of life and the course of evolution can enable oneself to sublimate the personal attachments into the universal and impersonal love.

Whatever may be its form, love there must be for the fulfilment of the ultimate destiny of the man. This is an expression of the universal brotherhood that exists between all the sentient beings; in fact, love is the objective realization of the subjective unity underlying everything that is manifested. It is said in *At the Feet of the Master* by J. Krishnamurti, the famous philosopher of the present age, that "Of all the Qualifications, Love is the most important, for if it is strong enough in a man, it forces him to acquire all the rest, and all the rest without it would never be sufficient". Love is essential for every aspirant. Indeed, there must be a flower before it is offered to the beloved or to the Lord. By unfolding this quality, by being more loving, by radiating human goodness as flowers radiate fragrance, the individual will be fulfilling his destiny which is to link the human with the Divine.

THE PERFECTED HUMANITY

By

SHRI J. P. SANJANA

Bombay Theosophical Federation

The Perfected Humanity has been referred to in almost all the scriptures of the world, both of the East and of the West. In the Hindu scriptures very high beings like *Brahma*, *Vishnu* and *Mahesh*, and again lesser deities like *Agni*, *Varuna* and others have been mentioned. In Jainism as many as twenty-four *Tirthankars* have been named, and detailed information is available for the last two of them. The last of the Thirthanakars had been the Lord Mahavira who lived in the same age as that of the Lord Buddha. Even the Sikhs eulogize Guru Nanak and others as the Great Masters, whom they consider as perfected humanbeings. The Jesus Christ is a Perfect Man among the Christians; other references are made suggesting St. John, St. Maichel and others as Perfect Men. Among the galaxy of Perfected Human-beings, the names of venerated ladies like Virgin Mary, Lady Fatima and *Jagadamba* (the World Mother) are mentioned, who have completed the lessons they had to learn as humanbeings and are helping humanity to evolve. Evidently, this concept of Perfected Humanity is neither new, nor Indian in its origin;

it is a universal concept which has prevailed throughout the ages.

At this stage, one may like to consider how far this idea of Perfected Humanity is rational ?

While considering our own humanity, we are struck by the range of disparity: on the one hand, there are idiots, savages and madmen; while on the other, there are statesmen, savants and geniuses. There are aborginals of Australia and Africa who even kill their beloved wives and devour their flesh with relish when they feel hungry. There are also cultured and educated men of the average type who study their lessons and earn their living. There are also though only a few, outstanding men like Albert Einstein, Jawaharlal Nehru and others, who are in the forefront of various human activities.

This idea of perfection is not exclusive only to human-beings ; even among the animals we find different grades of intelligence and understanding. Such differences are found among cats, dogs, elephants, monkeys and other animals. Different breeds of dogs, who have shown considerable understanding also suggest evolving consciousness within the same specie of the animal. If this gradation is evident in animals and men, why should we not assume that there may be a stage of perfection even for men, when they become Perfected Ones ?

Let us look at Science. The general trend of the scientific thought indicates that the principle of growth is a movement from simple to the complex, from homogeneous to the heterogeneous. Homogeneous means the coming together of identical parts; heterogeneous, the coming together of differing parts. Our various limbs do different work, yet they are combined together in the humanbeing. Thus, the physiological structure of the man also indicates that his is a very complex constitution. If men could have been considered as evolved from monkeys, why can we not think that there may be a stage beyond humanity as well ?

Anthropologically speaking there are different races, such as white or wheatish, yellow and black. These races show great differences in their physical, emotional and intellectual powers. Though the Negroes are showing signs of increasing sensitivity as expressed through painting, music etc., yet they have a very much developed physical nature. The yellow race had developed their emotional and intellectual qualities much more than the black races, but they have shown many signs of greater physical prowess than the Indian or the European race. Probably, this may also suggest that the qualities of analysis and criticism which are so much emphasized in the present day population may be superseded by other virtues which could be expressed by races which may follow. Even our children are showing much more critical faculties than we did in our childhood. This is evident in the questions they put to us. This by itself is an indication of some sort of evolutionary process. If this is so, it is just possible that there might perhaps be some other faculty, which need to be developed. The faculty of synthesis, which is being shown by some persons, like Sir James Jeans, Bertrand Russel and others, who are trying to synthesize knowledge in different fileds, is said to be the next higher faculty which would be developed by men. Beyond this, there is the faculty of intuition—the principle by which Truth is known in a flash, without too much of study and reading. That is a possibility any way. Thus, this growth in the consciousness of man could lead us to think of the possibility when men would know everything and be omniscient.

The most convincing proof of anything is considered to be the personal testimony. There are many persons who have come in close contact with the Mighty Beings who are perfect; they are also called the Elder Brethren, because of the stage in evolution which they have attained. Persons who have seen Yogi Aurobindo, Swami Ram Krishna or Swami Sivanand consider them to be very great masters. Similar sentiments have been expressed even about Ramanujacharya and others. In the present age, some of the Theosophical leaders like Madam H. P. Blavatsky, Rev. C. W. Leadbeater, Mrs. Annie Besant and others, as well as less known persons like Damodar K. Mavalanker and Shri Ramaswami Iyer had come into closer touch with Perfected Beings about whom they have written in detail. We may believe in the testimony of the persons with integrity of character. Any way, we may accept it as a probability that there is an evolutionary growth of men into Supermen, and that it may be possible for us to know Them. A sufi poet once said : "From mineral I awoke into the vegetable; from vegetable I awoke into the animal; from animal I awoke into man. When did I become less ?"

After all, what is the purpose of this humanity? Life from birth till death is both a drudgery and a tragedy. Every day we repeat mechanically the same diurnal routine without any sense of happiness or attainment. On the other hand, there is the point of view that life is full of joy. As is expressed by one writer, 'The soul of man is immortal, and its future is the future of a thing whose growth and splendour has no limit'. In India it is very commonly said that we are not our physical, emotional or mental bodies, rather we are *Atman*, the Immortal Spark of the Flame. From this *Atmic* stand-point we do not only say that perfection is a possibility, rather we say that it is our birth-right, specially because it is inherent in us. In one of the Sanskrit verses it is said : एको देव: सर्व भुतेषु गुढ:, सर्व व्यापी सर्व भुतांतरात्मा ।

The One Life hidden in all living beings, which pervades all, is the Inner Self of all. Again, it is said : *Tatwam Asi*, which means, That art thou. From this standpoint when we consider ourselves as souls, life is no more a drudgery and a tragedy, rather, the entire process is the process of onward movement to the glory of perfection. If we consider that we are souls, then the future glory of man is beyond debate. Even Al Mansur, a Muslim mystic has affirmed—*Anal Hak*, *Anal Hak*, which means 'I am That, I am That'.

What is the nature of a Perfect Man or the Adept ? The Adept or the Master has realized the one-ness of life. When the Perfected Man has realized the one-ness, He is one with the genius as well as with the idiot. This identity is not only on the physical level, it is so even on the supraphysical level. Secondly, the Adept is Omnipotent, Omnipresent, and Omniscient. His will can do and undo everything. Examples of such deeds are not wanting; practically all the scriptures are full of descriptions of such deeds. He is omnipotent in both time and space: sitting in the seclusion of the Himalayan mountains, He knows everything that is happening in any part of the globe. Similarly about time; He knows the future as well as the past. Time is not a veil, everything to Him is like an open book. His love is omnipresent. A mother's love for her child is well known, but the Master's love for each person whether he is an aborginal or a genius, whether he is black or brown, is more complete. His love for humanbeings is as intense as it is for minerals and vegetables, the living and the non-living. It is unfathomable in depth and limitless in expansion. There is a saying in the Bible that, "Come unto me all ye labour and are heavy laden and I will give you rest; for my yoke is easy and my burden light." The Lord Krishna says in *The Bhagwad Gita*, "Whatever you do......let it all be done for me as mine". Such is the love of the Master. The Master is Omniscient, as He knows all the knowledge of the past, the present and the future; He is so mericiful as to forgive all sins of ours.

The Master has developed all the eight *siddhies*. He can magnify as well as contract Himself to any extent. He can travel at will from one place to another, and He can also take a *Mayabi Roopa*, that is, He can materialize in any form He desires. He has not only attained a very high level of intellect, but He also has got very beautiful and perfectly healthy body. In fact, He has attained perfection in all the seven principles of which humanbeings are composed. It is interesting to note that the pure sense of humour, which does not ridicule anyone but makes light the heavy burden of every soul, is present in every Adept to a very great extent.

The Perfected Men do not live only in India. These Masters of the Wisdom have their consciousness linked with one another, though in geographical location they are situated at different places. They have their abodes in different places of the world. One of Them lives in the mountainous regions of China. He has a very tall body and looks after the evolution of the yellow race. There are others who reside in the pure tranquillity of the Himalayan mountains. The Lord Vaivasvata Manu stays on the southern slope of the Himalayas. The Lord Maitreya Bodhisattva also stays on the same side of the slope. There are many other Masters such as the Master Morya, the Master Koot Hoomi, and the Master Dwajkul who reside among the Himalayan mountains on the northern slope. That is why the Himalayas are considered as the spiritual home of the Great Beings. There is one Master who stays in South India: The Rishi Agastya stays among the Nilgiri Hills. In Egypt, there is the Luxor Brotherhood of Perfected Men. In Lebanon, there is an Adept who lives among one of the tribes and teaches them to live a more noble life. There is one Adept staying in Hungary who looks after the evolution of the European race. In the Central America, there is the Yucatan

Brotherhood which looks after the perfection of the Red Indians. There are many other Adepts but we do not know much about Them. These Adepts are not only the incharge of different geographical territories helping the perfection of the residents of these areas, but they are also responsible for different temperaments such as ritualistic, scientific, administrative and others. The Adept incharge of each temperament looks after the evolution and perfection of humanbeings who have that temperament irrespective of their location and nationality.

It may be natural at this point to enquire about the work of these Masters. What do They do for mankind ? They have got several types of work to do for the welfare of humanity. Though the progress of humanity in general is their concern, They do have certain special groups and specialized nature of work to perform as well. There are some Perfected Men, who are working on the Will aspect. These Masters who are working on the line of Will, look after the work of legislation, judiciary, army, administration and other similar activities. Those Elder Brethren who are working on the Wisdom line, look after the work of educational improvements and religious revivals. Some Teachers are helping science, arts, and other branches of human progress. All these Adepts are doing tremendous work on the spiritual planes as well as on other invisible planes. They are sending blessings at every moment to millions of people. They are pouring Their blessings on the invisible planes so that all sorts of life may get great impulse for their onward journey, their evolution to their ultimate destiny. Such impulses are received even by scientists and statesmen who get flashes of ideas for the furtherance of learning and social reorganizations. The Masters send Their help to scholars like Max Muller and others who go looking for old manuscripts and deciphering cave-edicts. When these scholars get stuck-up after their hard work and come to a dead-end in their studies, it is the impulse of these Great Ones that some keys to the mystery that had baffled them flash on their inwards eyes and the age old mystery in the twinkling of an eye is solved. These Great Ones also train humanbeings to share Their glorious responsibilities and to become useful channels for the Divine downpouring. These disciples are trained on the astral plane and teaching is imparted to them whenever it is needed. Very often, it is experienced that an individual troubled with numerous worries and anxieties sleep full of them, but when he gets up, he is lulled; the source of evil is still there but he finds some wonderful sense of comfort and relief. Such help is given generally by the trained disciples of the Masters. The Perfected Men have much to do on invisible planes and for that work They take helpers and disciples.

Such teachings about the Great Ones who have perfected themselves and belong to the Great White Brotherhood are not new. These teachings have remained concealed in almost every religion, but during the recent centuries persons like Madam H. P. Blavatsky, Mrs. Annie Besant, Bishop C. W. Leadbeater and others have reaffirmed the existence of such Great Beings. The knowledge has always been present but if we take more interest in Them and Their work, we shall know more about Them. This understanding, however, should not be merely armchair understanding. It is only by noble living, pure life and helpful activities that we may come nearer the Occult Hierarchy and the Perfected Beings. It is only by coming closer to Them that we can know more about Them and serve the humanity in an effective way.

GLOSSARY

Agni : Fire goddess

Ahimsā : Non-violence

Atmā : Soul (Cf. Man)

Avidyā : Ignorance

Bhāgavad Gitā: The song of the Lord; a scripture of the Hindus

Brahmā : God the Creater (Cf. Logos)

Chakrās : Force centres : Seven in number, which arise in the etheric portion of the nerve centres within the spine and terminate in circular depression. Each *chakram* performs dual function within the body. It absorbs life and energy and also acts as a transformer by means of which vital forces generated within the body are changed in intensity so that they can be expressed through a denser vehicle. One such centre is at the back of the body over the extreme lower end of the spine. It is specialized to absorb the force known as the *Kundalini Shakti* (q. v.) that emanates from the Earth and gives life to the organs of the body. (For details please see *The Chakras* : C. W. Leadbeater).

Ego : Self; the unified triad, Atma-Buddhi-Manas, or the duad, Atma-Buddhi ; that immortal part of man which reincarnates and gradually progresses to the final goal—*Nirvana*. Also the consciousness in man—'I am I'—or the feeling of 'I-am-ship'. Esoteric philosophy teaches the existence of two Egos in man, the mortal or personal, and the Higher, the Divine or the Impersonal, calling the former "Personality" and the latter "Individuality".

Guru : Teacher. A member of the Adept Brotherhood (Cf. Occult Hierarchy) who accepts disciples and guides them to attain Perfection. These Teachers have themselves attained Perfection and have acquired various *siddhies*. They have transcended the wheel of births and deaths but have elected themselves to be with the Humanity to help 'God's Plan which is evolution'. (For details please see *The Masters and the Path* : (C. W. Leadbeater).

Indra : A Hindu god who is supposed to rule the heaven world.

Jagadambā : The World Mother. A member of the Adept Brotherhood (Cf. Occult Hierarchy). She looks after women, children and the sick. She attends to all child-births in a mysterious way, and aids the pregnant mothers in their trial.

Jāmun : A berry-like fruit got from a big tree.

Jeevānu : Life-atoms; the carrier of Life-force.

Karma : Action; Cause and effect. The Law of Karma guides the entire creation. There are three types of *Karmas*, viz. *Sanchita* (accumulated), *Prārabdha* (starting) and *Agāmi* or *Kriyamāna* (future). These operate over the individual as well as on different groups and nations. The Lords of Karma adjust the various forces generated by the individual and the groups in such a way that the individual or the group could evolve successively through many lives, so that ultimately, the destined archetype is attained.

Kundalini Shakti: The Serpent Fire. This force is at present unknown to science. Three types of energy viz., Prāna, Fohāt and *Kundalini* surround us. Prāna comes to us directly from the sun. Fohāt is the energy of the Cosmic Logos. *Kundalini Shakti* or the Serpent Fire comes from the Earth and affects the physical construction of the dense body, giving it health and vigour. This force is absorbed by the Root Chakram (q.v.). After absorption and internal action, the Serpent Fire rises up the Spine and is distributed throughout the nerves of the body. It also acts upon the blood-stream and the sex organs. (For details please see *The Etheric Double* : A. W. Powell).

Lajjābati : A small plant which contracts from human touch.

Logos : One Universal Life; God. The universe is the expression of a Conscious Life. This One Life is a Person but He transcends all the limitations which necessarily are associated with our ideas of Personality. Cosmic Logos is ever a Unity, 'One without a second', nevertheless, as He energizes the universe, He energizes it as a Trinity of the three fundamental modes of manifestations. God as a Trinity is described in Hinduism as *Brahmā* the Creater, *Vishnu* the Preserver, and *Shivā* the Destroyer.

Mahesh : Lord Shivā; the God of Destruction (Cf. Logos)

Man : Triple in constitution : Spirit, Soul and Body or Monad, Ego and Personality. The Monad sends out a Ray which is also triple in manifestation : Atma, Buddhi and Manas. These three constitute the Ego (q.v.) of the man, which in its turn sends out a Ray which is consciousness working through the Mental, Emotional and Physical bodies. This triad is known as his Personality. (For details please see *Man and His Bodies* : Annie Besant).

Mayābi Roopa : Illusory Form; 'materialization' at will for specific purpose.

Occult Hierarchy: There is a band of Adept workers who carry out God's Plan for this globe. This Brotherhood is an association of Supermen; it is a living organism which contains the Life-energies of the Logos (q.v.). The Adepts of the Great White Brotherhood work in true hierarchical order, according to their qualifications, each having his work in a particular department of the Plan.

Panchāyat : The rule by the five elders of the village

Purushottama : Higher Being (Cf. Man)

Sākshi : Witness; the Silent Watcher

Sallabha : Easy

Samsāra : The World

Siddhies : Attainments. When different *chakrās* (q. v.) are energized, the individual attains various psychic powers known as the *siddhies*.

Sutrās : Aphorisms

Tirthankaras : Succession of Jain Masters of which the Lord Mahavira was the latest. Lord Mahavira was a contemporary of Gautam Buddha.

Vamana : A Hindu deity

Vāyu : God of air

Vidyā : Wisdom, Knowledge

Vishṇu : God the Preserver

Yagna : Sacrificial ritual

INDEX